Oleg Pomoshnikov

The Russian Missile Destroyer of Project 61 (Kashin Class) 1962

KAGERO

The first ship of the series, with short fore funnel. Port side view.

Large ASW ship Kashin class (Project 61)

"Singing frigates", "Greyhounds of the Oceans" – each of this names contains a little bit of truth about large anti-submarine warfare ships Project 61. Since their emergence until now they are very popular with both: maritime specialists and shiplovers. It could not be otherwise, because they are exceptionally good looking vessels. They were first Soviet units of the new generation, projected and built separate from foregoing schemes. Their uniqueness was not only based on beautiful architecture, but also on some other assets. First of all they were first ships in the world propelled only by the power of gas turbines.

Landmark project

After years of building the ships based on the improved pre-war projects it was a time for making the landmark. During the second half of the fifties constructors started to project ships which quality should surpass the predecessors. In 1956 the construction of new escort vessel, as it was originally classified, had begun. It had much stronger AA armament in comparison to Project 50 (Gornostaj, NATO code: Riga) and could sail with much higher speeds. Technical Order for projecting new ships was approved on 30th of April, 1957. Initial project was confirmed on 18th of September, 1957. The Central Construction Bureau No. 53 (CKB-53) at Leningrad was chosen as the main contractor of the new project, designated as Proj. 61. The main constructor was the young and talented engineer Boris Izrailevich Kupiensky (1916–1982). Technical project was finished on March, 1958. Its official approval took place on 15th of August, 1958.

Smooth deck and four funnels

Ships had a characteristic, slender silhouette and smooth deck with highly raised upper deck in bow section, and slightly raised stern. Ship's hull was fully welded, and made of low alloy structural steel type SChL-4 (10ChSND). Important feature of the construction was its continuous corridor (so called "stormy"), running through the whole length of the superstructures, which allowed the crew to move around with-

Starboard side view.

out leaving the ship's interior. Corridor was connected with almost every fighting position. Long complex of superstructures, trailing through 2/3 of deck's length, was made mainly from the light aluminum and magnesium alloys type AMG-5W.

Another, very characteristic feature were four short and wide funnels channeling hot combustion gasses from turbines. The shape and size of the funnels mantles allowed changing the turbines of the M-3 and GTU-6 generators by quickly opening the hatches placed near the chimneys. It also allowed to cool down the gasses to decrease the thermal vision spectrum. The new thing on Soviet ship was to separate the main command post from the bridge, and locating it inside, on lower deck.

"Singing turbines"

The Project 61 ships were first large vessels propelled only by gas turbines. The power plant consisted of two turbo gas generators M-3 of 36.000 hp each. Every generator had two turbo gas engines type M8E (DN59) of 18.000 hp each, and single-staged reversing gearing RB54, which allowed the connection and disconnection of any turbo gas engine by special friction claw-type and hydraulic clutches. Thanks to that it was possible to higher the economics of the generators on slow speeds. Except for summing up the power of two gas engines, the reducer ensured the reversion of the propeller from full ahead to full reverse, and vice versa. The propeller shafts were making 300 revolutions per minute on maximum speed. Overall power of the power plant was 72.000 hp. Generators transmitted the propulsion by side shafts to two 4-bladed propellers of 3,9 m in diameter.

Armament

The Project 61 vessels were armed with two close range AA rocket complexes type M-1 Volna, which were a counterparts of the S-125 Neva land versions. Each of them consisted of two-railed, stabilized, revolving launcher type ZIF-101. Fire unit consisted of 32 missiles. Each launcher had its own rocket storage with 16 projectiles (15 warheads and 1 trainer). Fire control for both M-1 complexes was ensured by two control systems Yatagan (4R90). In years 1965–1968 the first moderniza-

The ship, with a standart high bow funnel. Port side view.

tion of the M-1 Volna took place. The complex received the new type of missile then – the W-601 – with ceiling increased up to 15.000 meters and range up to 42 km.

The artillery armament consisted of two dual universal AK-726 guns cal. 76mm/59 (ZIF-67). Fire unit was 600 rounds per barrel. Fire control was ensured by two artillery radars MR-105 Turiel 61.

Standard ASW armament was a 5-pipe torpedo launcher cal. 533mm type PTA-53-61 located on the superstructure's roof. Ships also had 4 anti-submarine rocket launcher Smerch-2 (12 × 212mm) and Smerch-3 (6 × 300mm). They were also capable of taking one ASW Ka-25PL helicopter on board. There was a special helipad at the stern part of the vessel. The big disadvantage was a lack of hangar, though.

Whole series of Project 61 ships was planned for 20 units. They were built in two shipyards: No. 445 Shipyard named after 61 Communards in Mykolayiv and No. 190 Shipyard named after A.A. Zhdanov in Leningrad. Most of the units – 15 – were built in the first mentioned factory.

Right after entering the service of the first new ships the lack of strike capabilities came out. In 1969 the decision about modernization was made and vessels were going to receive anti-ship missiles and enforced AA and anti-missile defense systems. The modernization was quite complex and consisted of such features: installation of the anti-ship winged P-15M missiles launch unit; enforcing the anti-missile and AA defense capabilities with four 30mm AK-630 units with fire control systems; replacing the hydro-acustic station with Platin complex which used dragged antenna of variable submersion depth; increasing the ship's autonomy and range.

The main armament of such modernized units (61M/MP) were two fixed and non-stabilized containers KT-97M located at the stern. They consisted of anti-ship missiles P-15M Termit-M with Koral-NK rocket fire control system. Containers were set frontally towards the stern. On both sides in front of stern's funnels two pylons were placed as a base for two direct AA stations consisting of two six-barreled AK-630 guns cal. 30mm each. The last unit of the series – Sderzhanny – was finished with such specification. After that five more units were also modernized that way.

Next modernized vessel was Provornyy. The modernization was based on project 61E (experimental) and its purpose was to test new, universal, multichannel medium range missile complex M-22 Uragan and radiolocating station MR-700 Fregat. Missiles and radar were planned to be used on new destroyers Project 956 Sarych. The project of the new version was developed under the direction of B.I. Kupiensky during the period from the 22nd of August, 1973 to the 27th of August, 1974.

The most long-lived unit from all of the "Singing Frigates" was Smetlivy (year of build 1969). The modernization (according to the proj. 01090) was planned for two years, but it was realized in four times longer period. Project predicted an installation of the newest maritime,

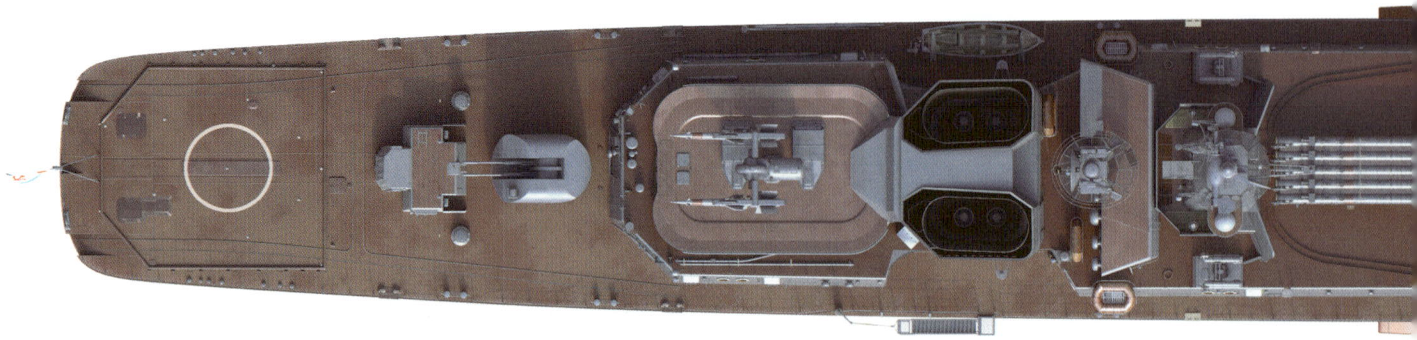

non-acustic submarine detection system MNK-300 Kayra, as well as anti-ship winged-missile launchers 3M24 Uran.

In 1974 Naval Command of India decided to buy modern destroyers. In the same year the delegation from that country visited the Soviet Union. The Indians were interested in buying the cheapest possible oceanic vessel which could escort their aircraft carrier. The choice went on Project 61. Works on the technical documentation of the project were conducted in 1975. Hull was lengthened up to 146.2 m and widened in the bow section were the anti-ship missile launchers should be placed. At the end of the stern the helipad (10 × 12 m), elevated to the superstructure level, was located. It allowed to operate one ASW Ka-25PL helicopter. In front of the helipad there was a partly immersed hangar for the helicopter. The whole feature demanded the removal of the stern's dual AK-726 gun, as well as radiolocating fire control system MR-105 Turiel. There was also no more space for mine rails and both rocket depth charges launchers RBU-1000. The main difference against the base project was the installation of the four single anti-ship missiles launchers in bow section. Vessels received the export version of P-15 missiles, designated as P-20M (Termit E). Two reliable cal. 76mm guns placed in the single turret stayed at the bow section. At the stern, on both of its sides, two batteries (2 × 2) of dual AK-230 guns were placed on pylons. Main AA armament was unchanged and it consisted of two universal Volna-M complexes. Thanks to the hangar on first three units it was possible to storage the Ka-25 helicopter. A total of five ships were built under the 61ME project.

Most of the 20 Soviet large ASW ships Proj. 61 were meant to serve on North, but the military situation enforced to leave many of them in Black Sea Fleet. Their main service waters was Mediterranean Sea. It is where the American airmen gave them the nickname of "Singing Frigates" because of the characteristic sound of working turbines.

Technical data of Komsomolets Ukrainy destroyer

Parameter	
Dimensions, m – max. length (water line) – max. width (water line) – sides height from base line, at bow/midships/stern	 143,95/131,96 15,78/13,99 13,19/8,08/8,49
Displacement, t – standard – normal – full load	 3400 3850 4300
Draft – at standard displacement – at full displacement	 3,83 4,46
Propulsion – power, hp	4 gas turbines 72.000
Armament – missiles – artillery – ASW	2 × 2 M-1 Volna (32 missiles) 2 × 2 cal. 76.2 mm guns 1 × 5 torpedo launchers cal. 533mm 2 × RBU 6000 2 × RBU 1000
Electronic equipment	2 × MR-300 Angara 1 × MG-312 Titan 1 × MG-311 Vychegda

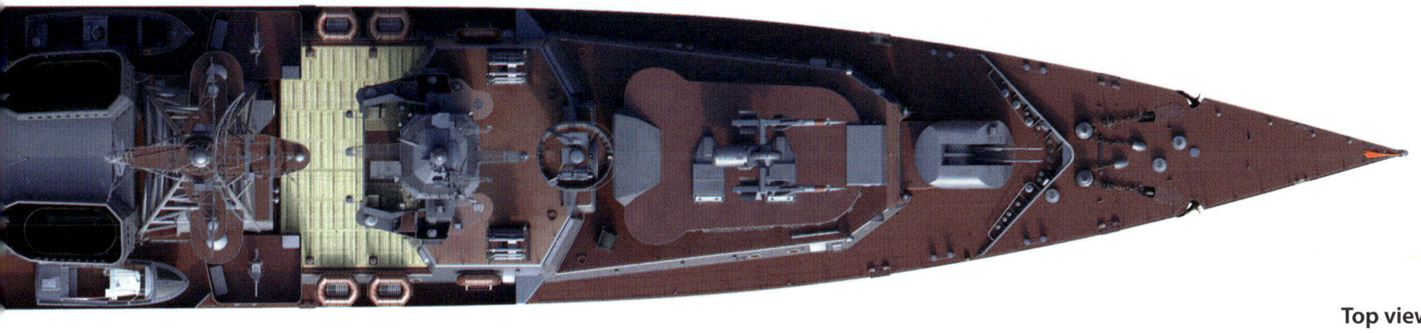

Top view.

Bow view.

Stern view.

Port side view of the bow with AK-726 bow turret.

The same but starboard view.

Bow M-1 "Volna" anti-aircraft missile launcher and the base of the conning tower.

Same thing but starboard view.

Port side view of the conning tower with Yatagan 4R-90 missile control radar. In front of the conning tower is the antenna post of the MR-105 artillery radar.

Starboard view of the conning tower.

Port side view of the bow funnel area.

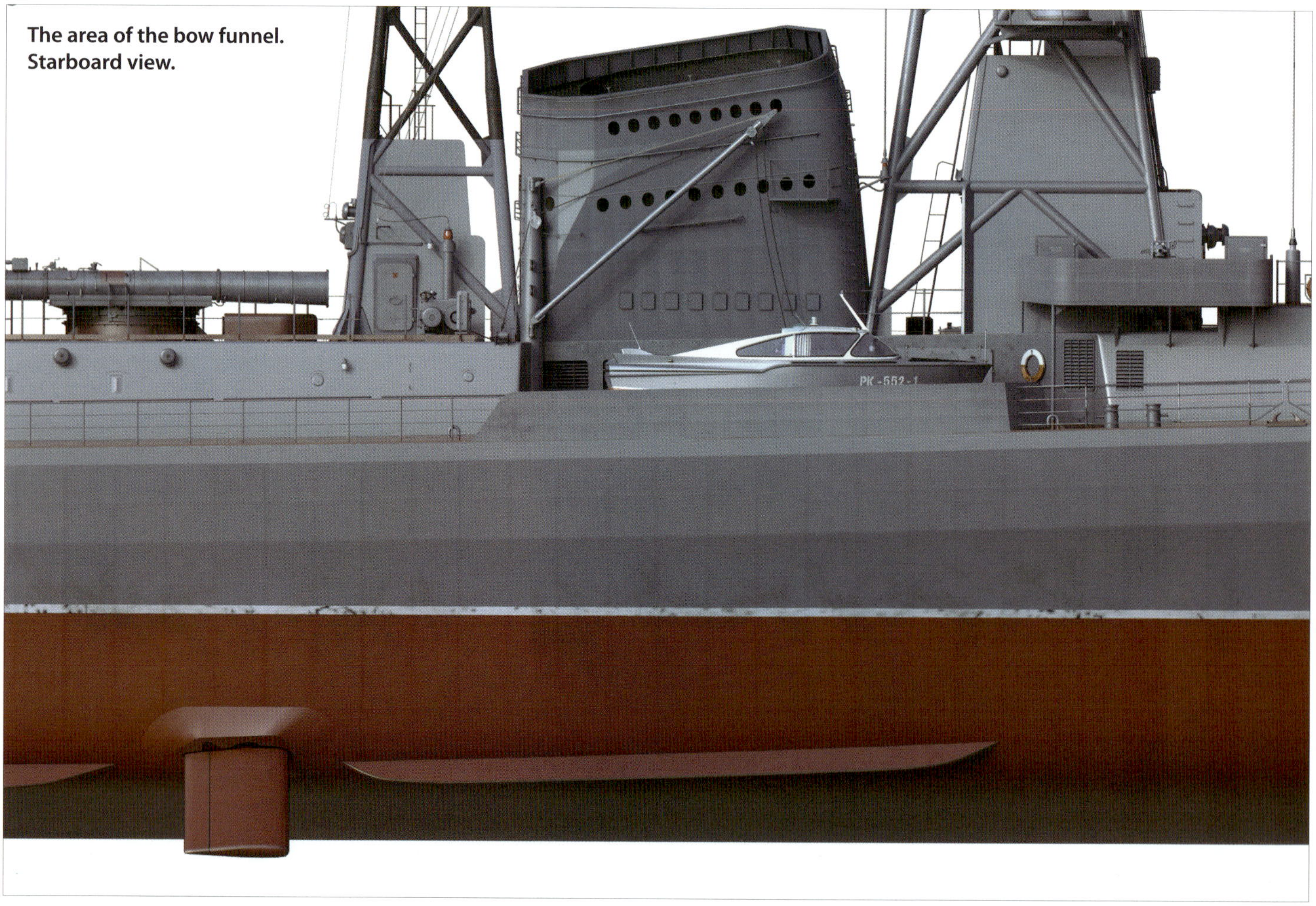

The area of the bow funnel. Starboard view.

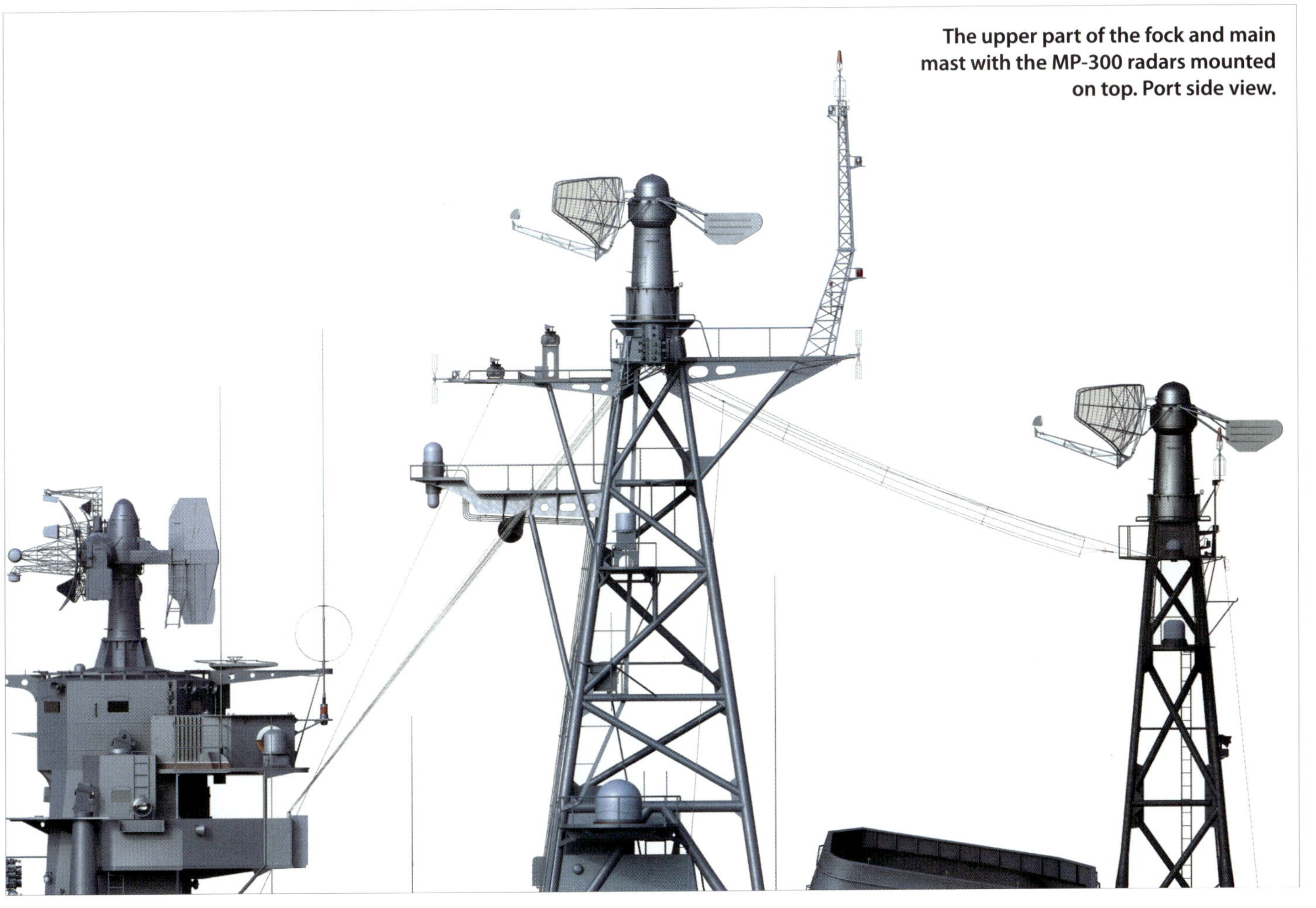

The upper part of the fock and main mast with the MP-300 radars mounted on top. Port side view.

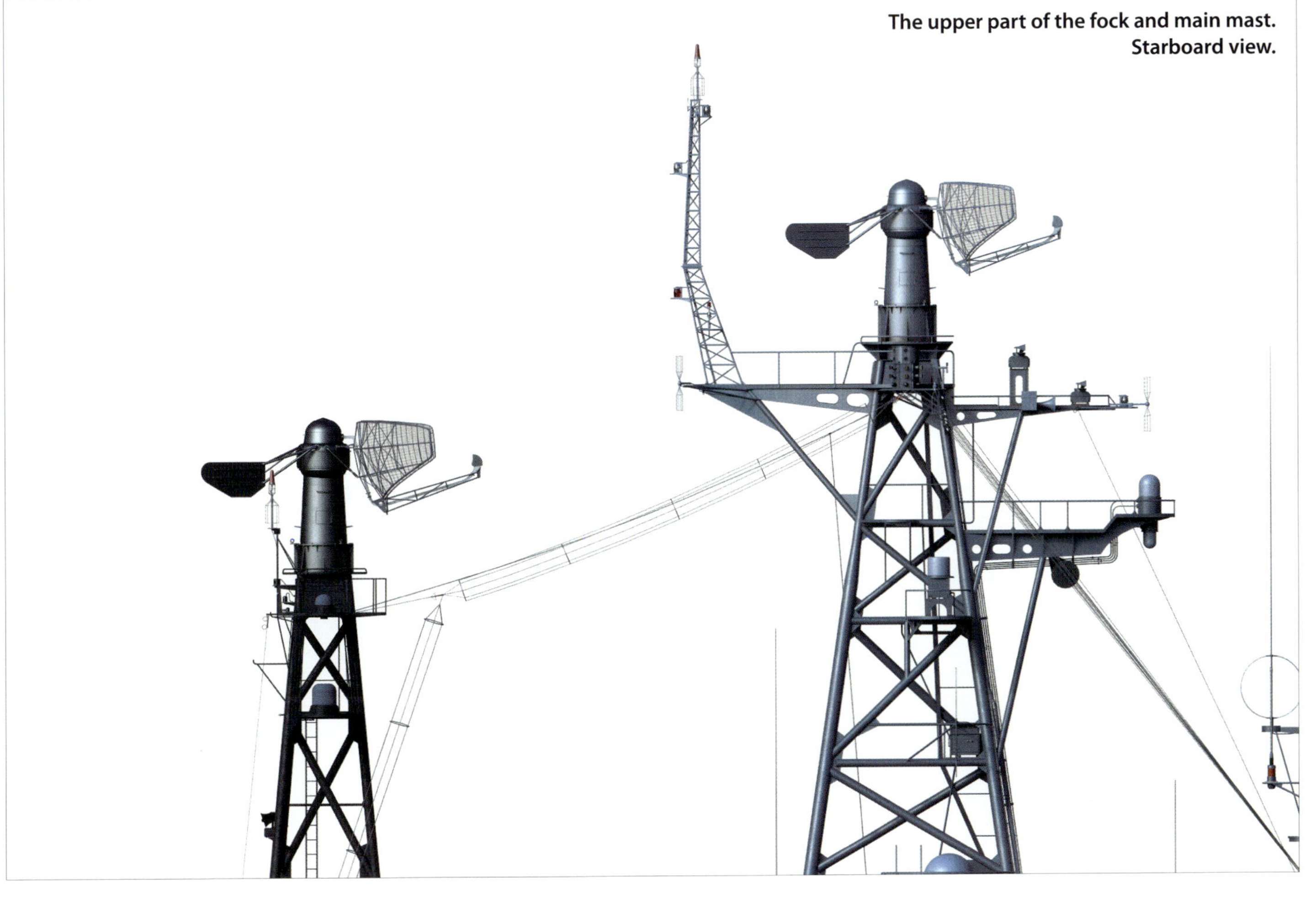

The upper part of the fock and main mast. Starboard view.

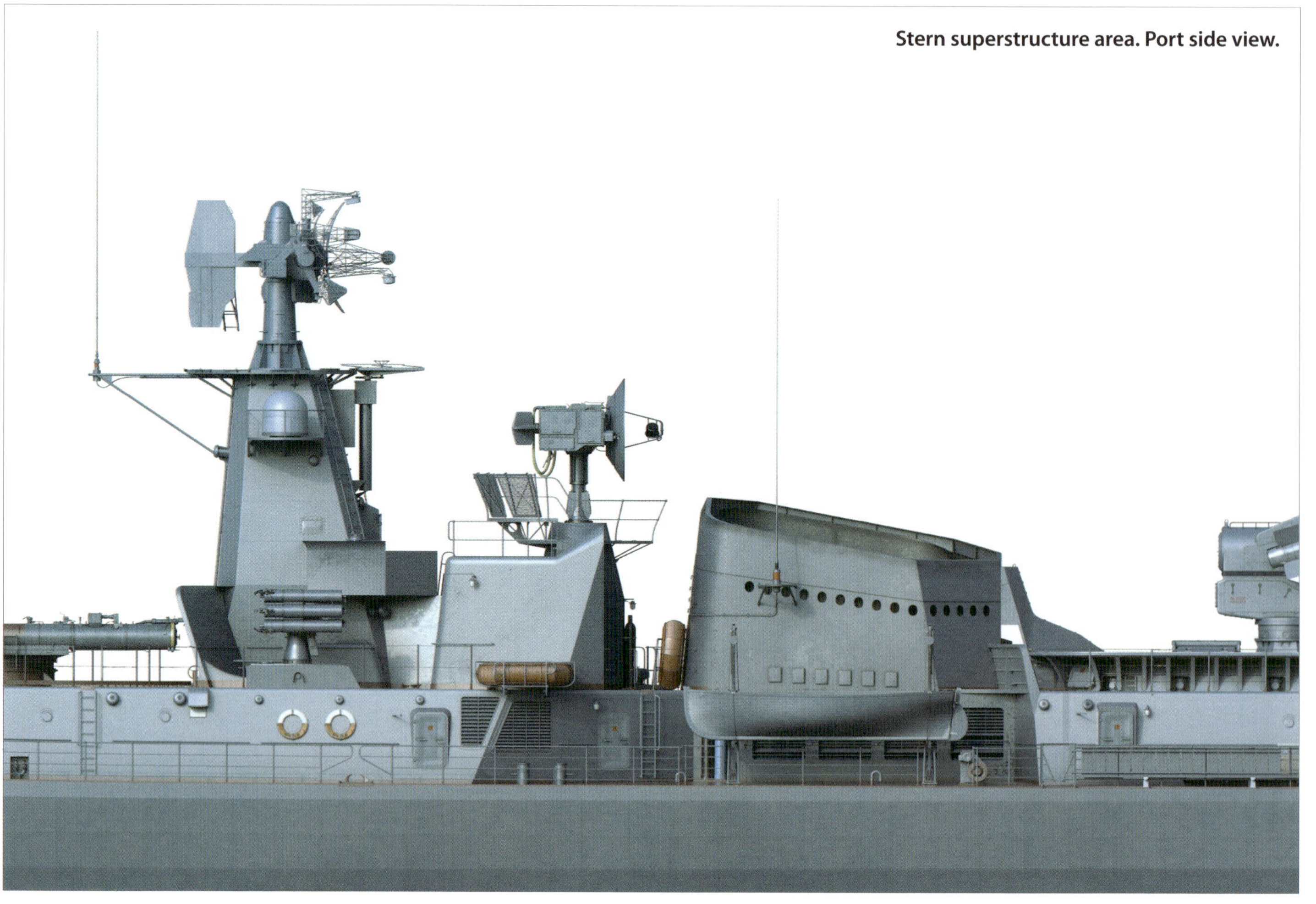

Stern superstructure area. Port side view.

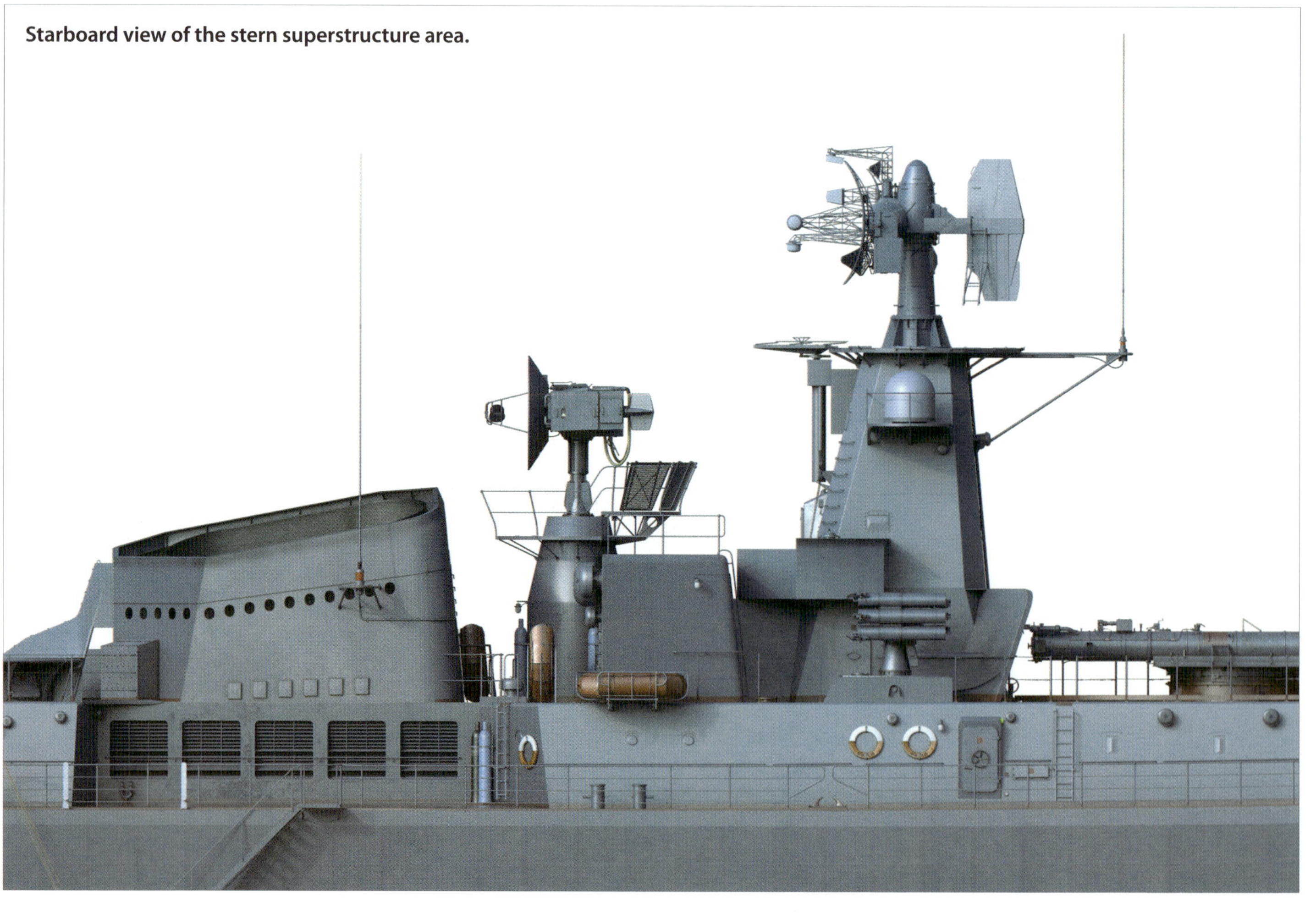

Starboard view of the stern superstructure area.

Stern M-1"Volna" anti-aircraft missile launcher & AK-726 turret. Port side view.

Starboard view of the stern M-1 "Volna" anti-aircraft missile launcher & AK-726 turret.

Stern of the ship. Port side view.

Starboard view of the stern.

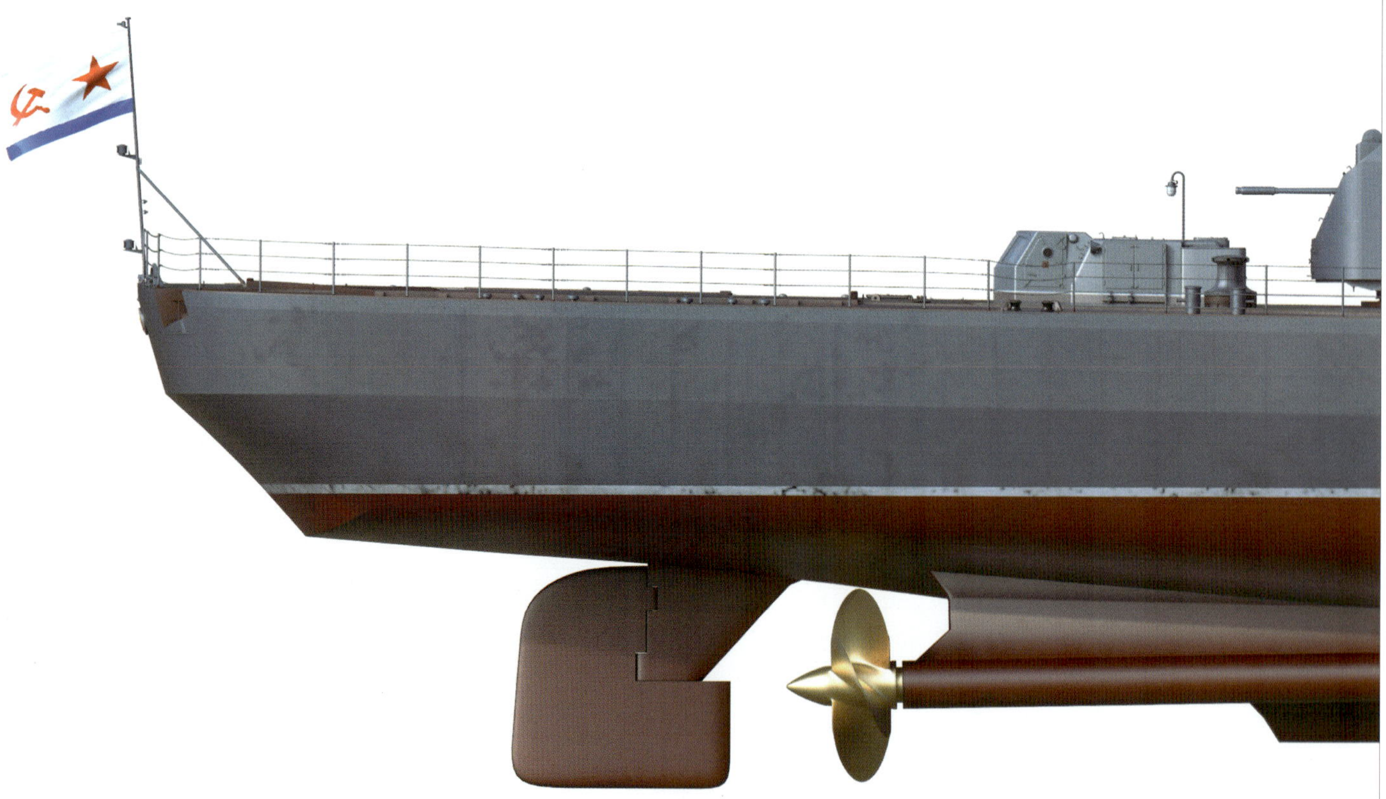

Top view of the foredeck & bow turret.

Top view of the fore M-1 "Volna" anti-aircraft missile launcher & bow superstructure.

Midship.

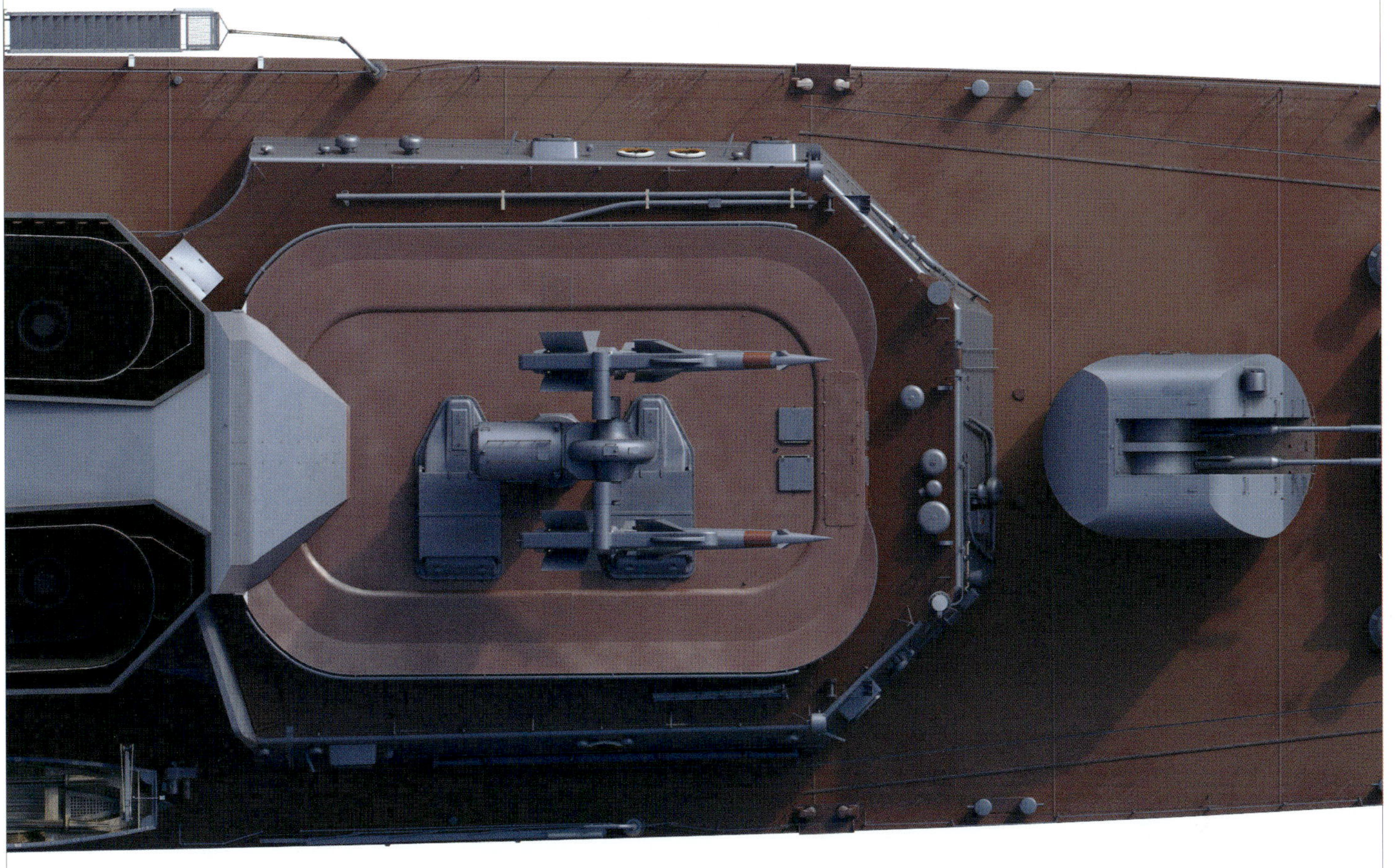

Top view of the rear funnel, M-1 "Volna" anti-aircraft missile launcher & stern AK-726 turret.

Top view of the of the stern.

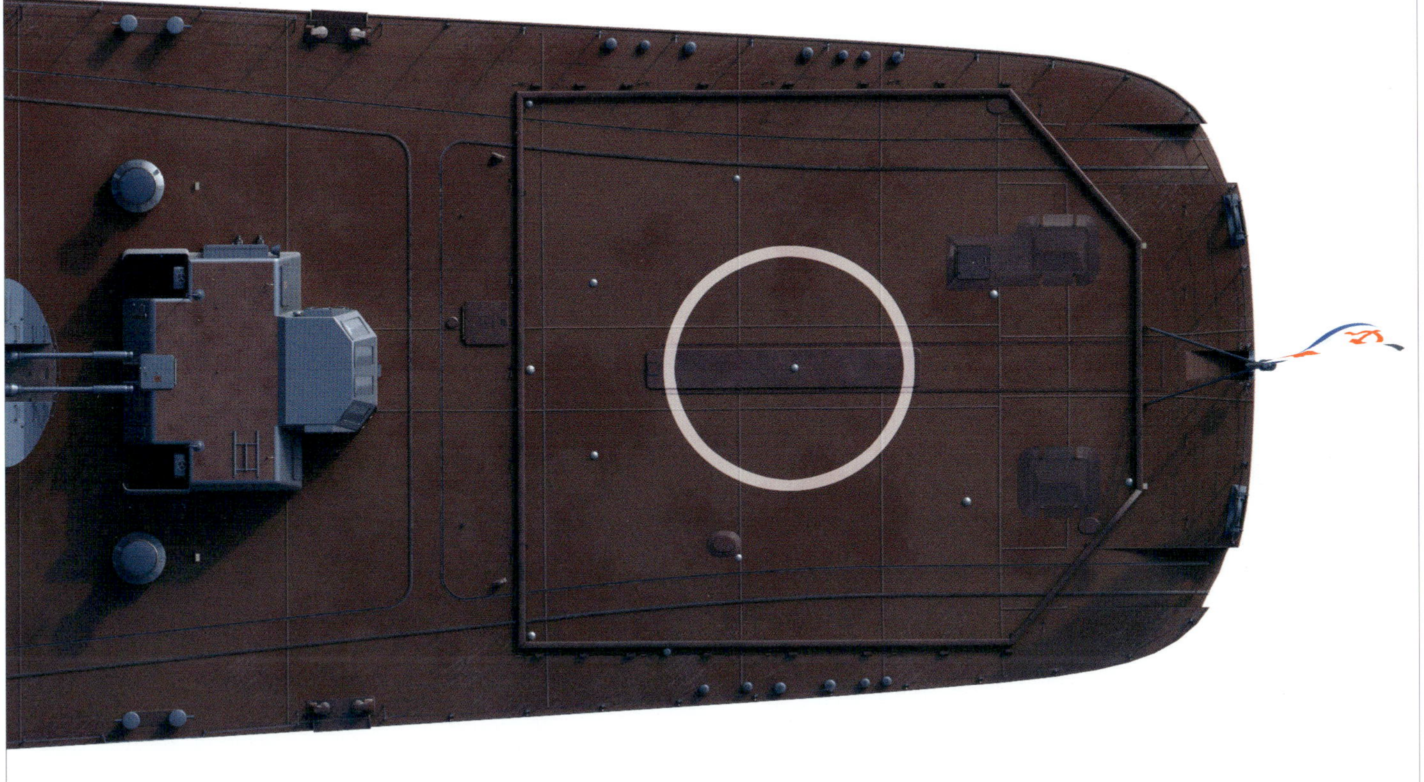

Foredeck.

Bow view on capstans & AK-726 76mm gun mount.

The bow section of the vessel as seen from above.

Starboard anchor & fairlead.

Starboard view on capstans, anchor chain stopper & anchor chain.

This view from above shows the breakwater.

Starboard part of the breakwater. Stern view.

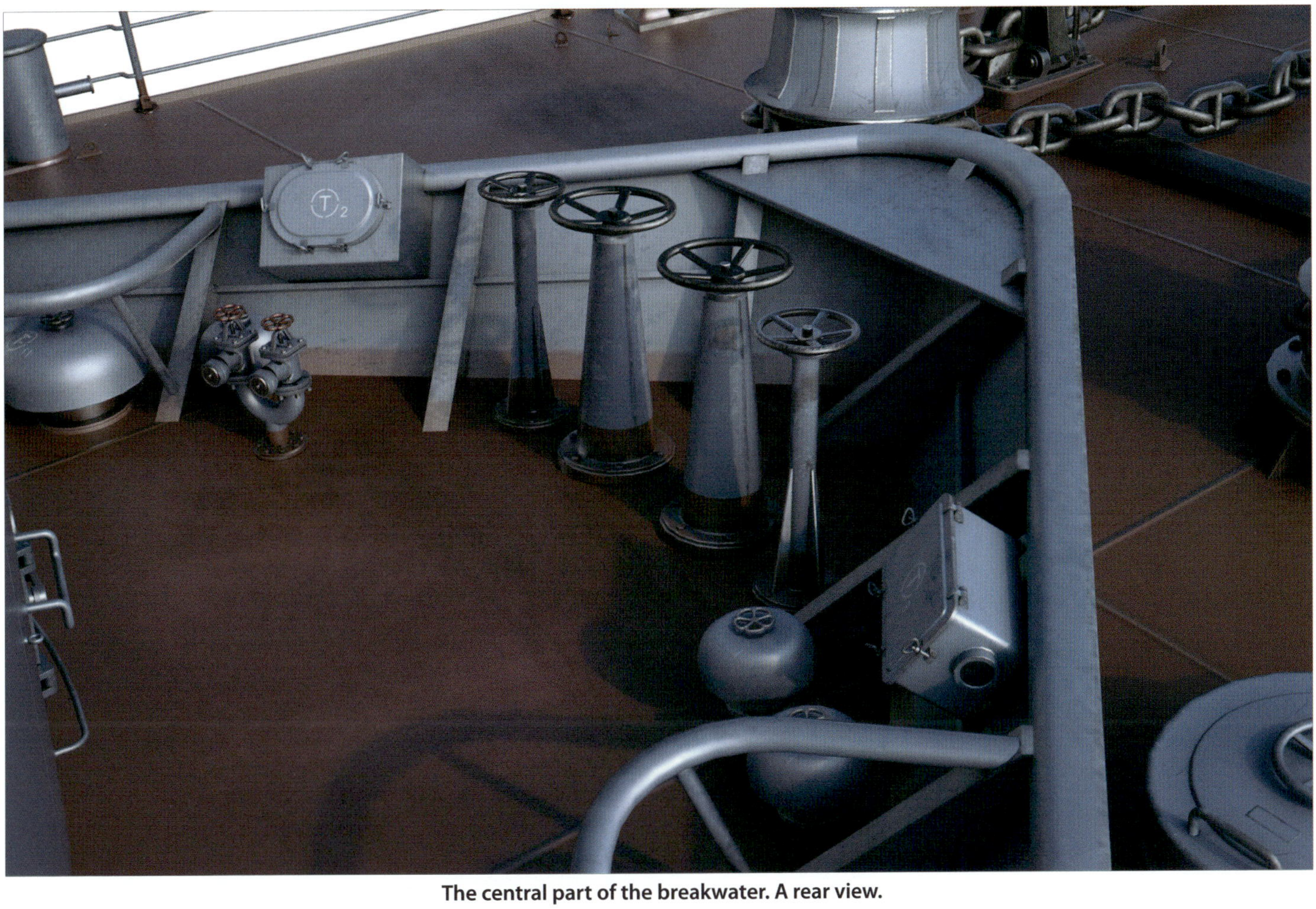

The central part of the breakwater. A rear view.

Port side part of the breakwater. Stern view.

Bow AK-726 76mm gun mount. Starboard view.

Bow part of the first tier superstructure. Starboard view from the bow. The bow starboard strut of the ship-to-ship cargo transfer system is clearly visible.

Bow part of the first tier superstructure. Starboard view from the bow. The bow starboard strut of the ship-to-ship cargo transfer system is clearly visible.

Port side view of bow part of superstructure.

Port side view of bow part of superstructure.

Bow ZIF-101 SAM "Volna".
Port side view.

A bird's eye view from the bow at the fore M-1 "Volna" anti-aircraft missile launcher.

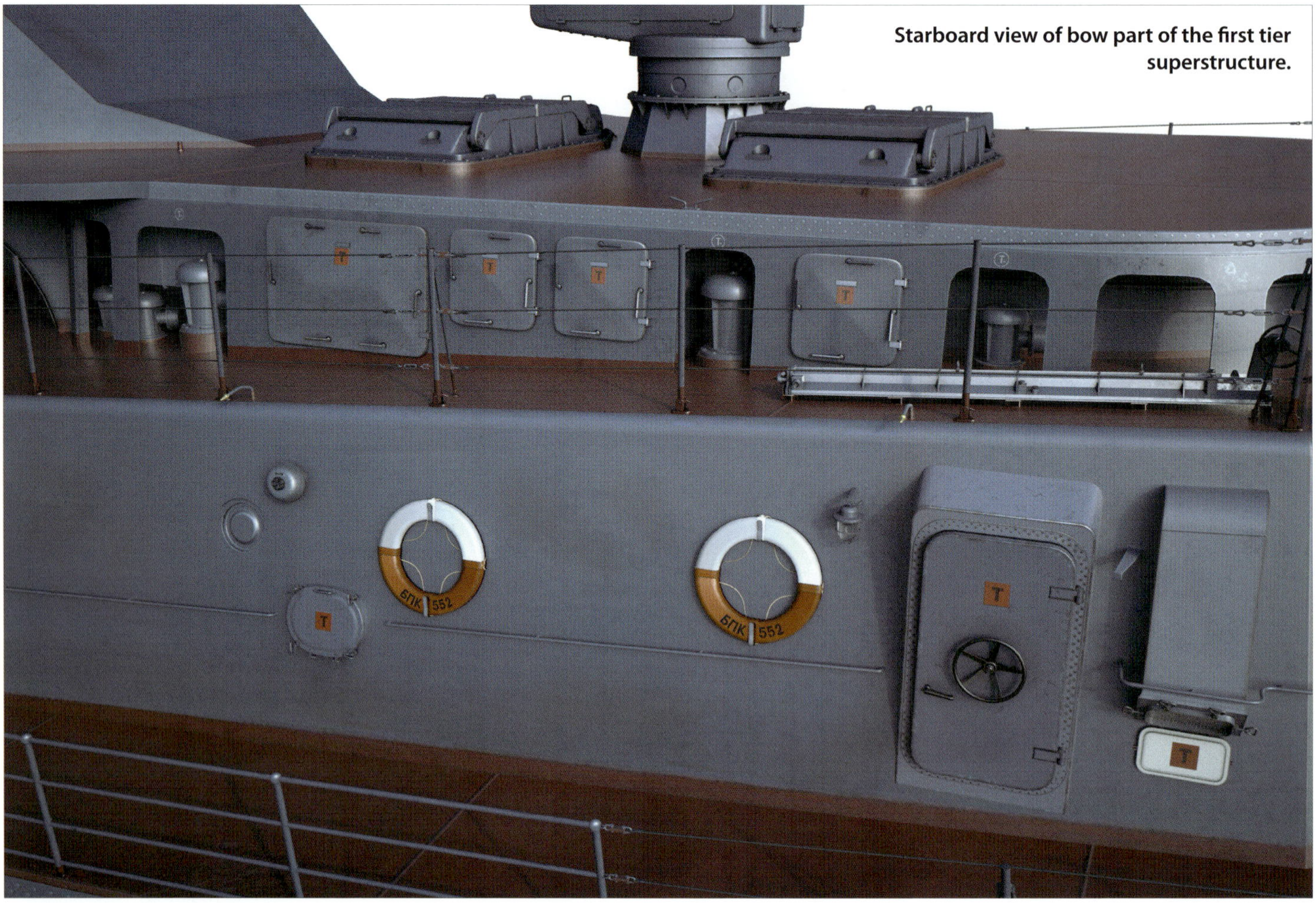

Starboard view of bow part of the first tier superstructure.

Starboard view of the fore part of the second tier superstructure, barbette of the MR-105 "Turel" artillery radar & and rocket gas reflector.

Starboard view of the fore part of second tier superstructure, barbette of the MR-105 "Turel" artillery radar & and rocket gas reflector.

Rear view of the rocket platform. Starboard side.

The front of the rocket platform. Starboard side.

Rear view of the rocket platform. Port side.

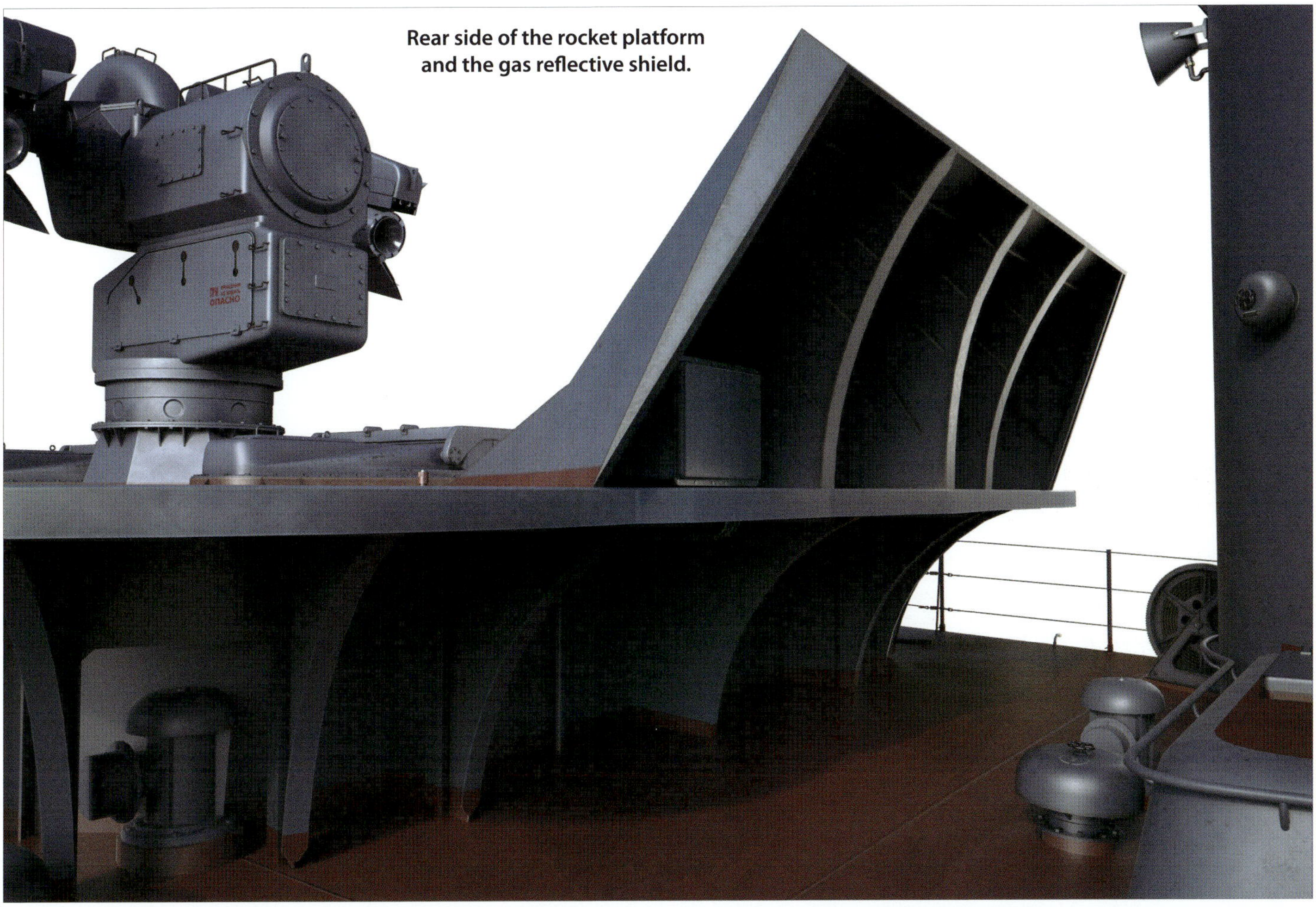

Rear side of the rocket platform and the gas reflective shield.

Port side wave guard with door. Rear view.

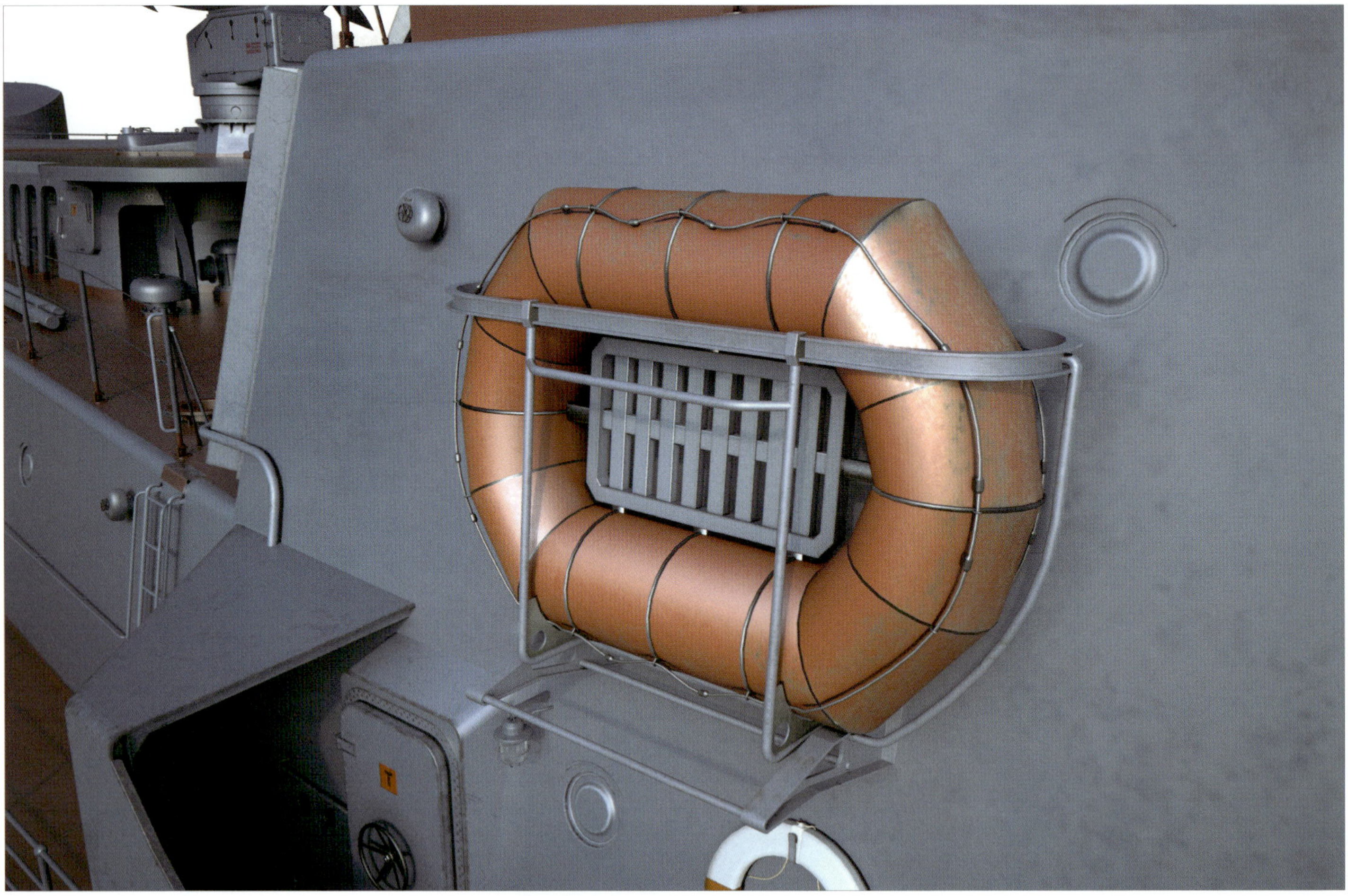

Port side of the second tier superstructure and life raft.

Port side RBU-6000 depth charge rocket launcher. Rear view.

Port side RBU-6000 depth charge rocket launcher. Fore view.

Port side rear view of the barbette of the MR-105 "Turel" artillery radar.

Port side view of the bow MR-105 "Turel" artillery radar.

Bow view of the fore MR-105 "Turel" artillery radar.

Starboard side wave guard with door. Rear view.

Starboard view of the conning tower base.

Starboard view on signal bridge of the conning tower.

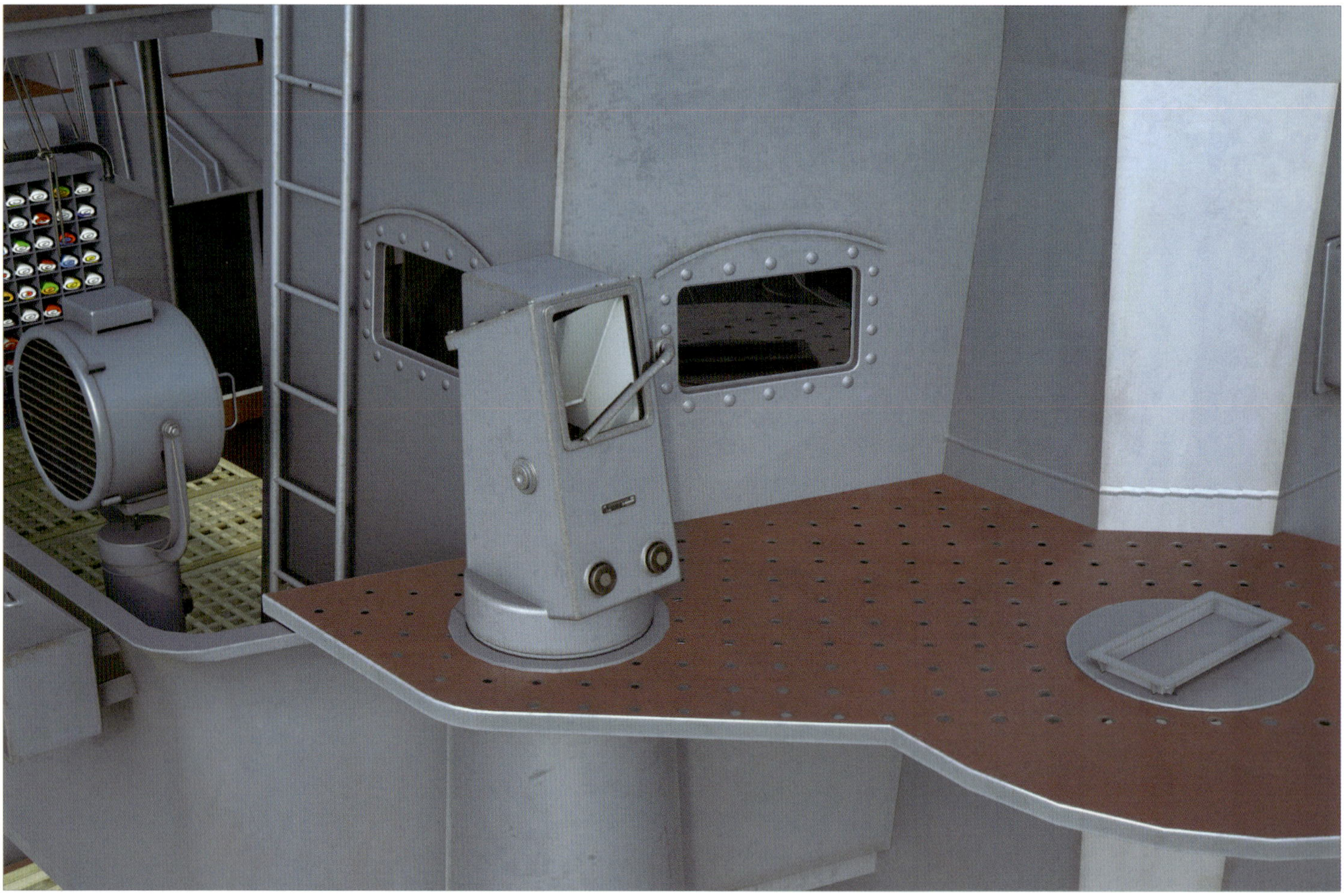
Starboard view on the periscope observation device.

Signal bridge. View from the stern.

Signal bridge. View to the port side.

Port side of the signal bridge. View from stern.

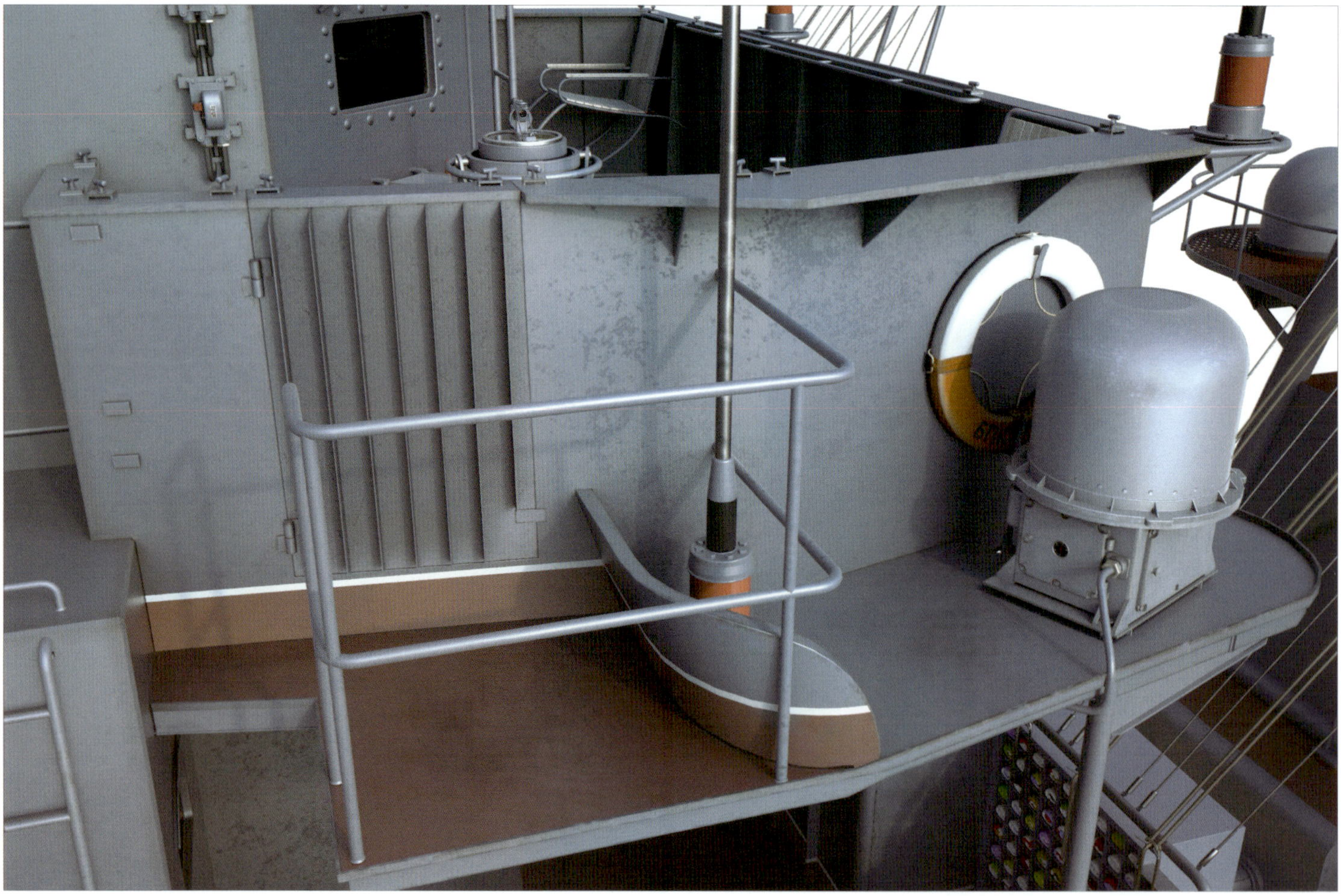

Port side view on the commander's bridge. To the right there is an antenna of station interference "CRAB-11".

Front of the commander's bridge. Port side bow view.

The conning tower top with "Yatagan" 4R-90 missile control radar.

The top of bridge superstructure with "Yatagan" radar as seen from above.

Starboard view on commander's bridge details.

Commander's bridge.

Commander's bridge.

Commander's bridge.

Rear view of the second tier superstructure & conning tower base.

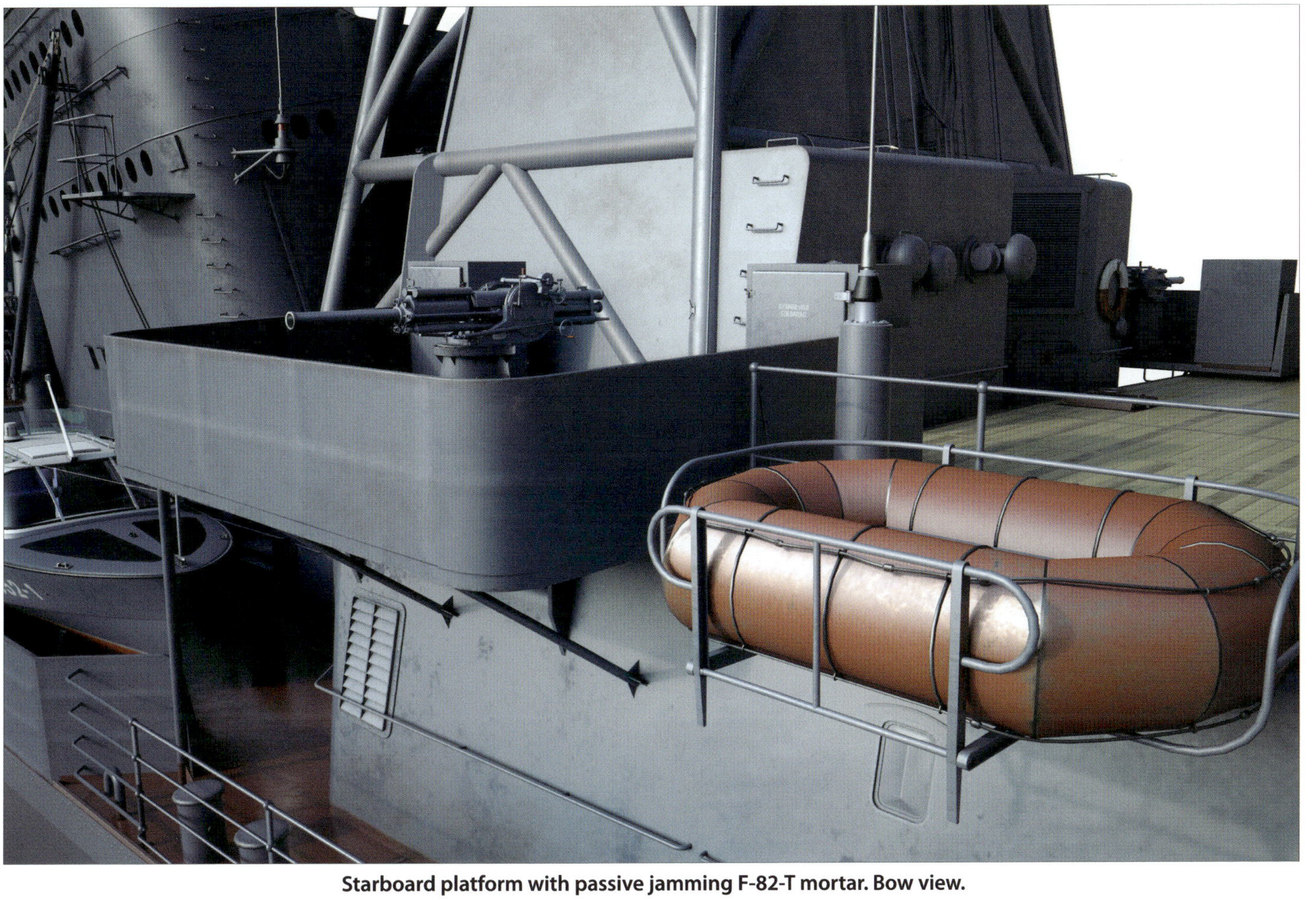

Starboard platform with passive jamming F-82-T mortar. Bow view.

A bird's eye view from starboard side of the passive jamming F-82-T mortar platform & the fore mast base.

First tier of the fore mast with "CRAB-12" antenna post.

Second tier of the fore mast with radio antenna. Port side view.

Third and fourth tier of fore mast. Port side view.

Third tier of fore mast with the port side "CRAB-11" antenna of station interference.

Third tier of fore mast with the port side "CRAB-11" antenna of station interference.

Fourth tier of fore mast with antenna post of the electronic intelligence station "Zaliv". Port side view.

Port side view of the fore mast masthead.

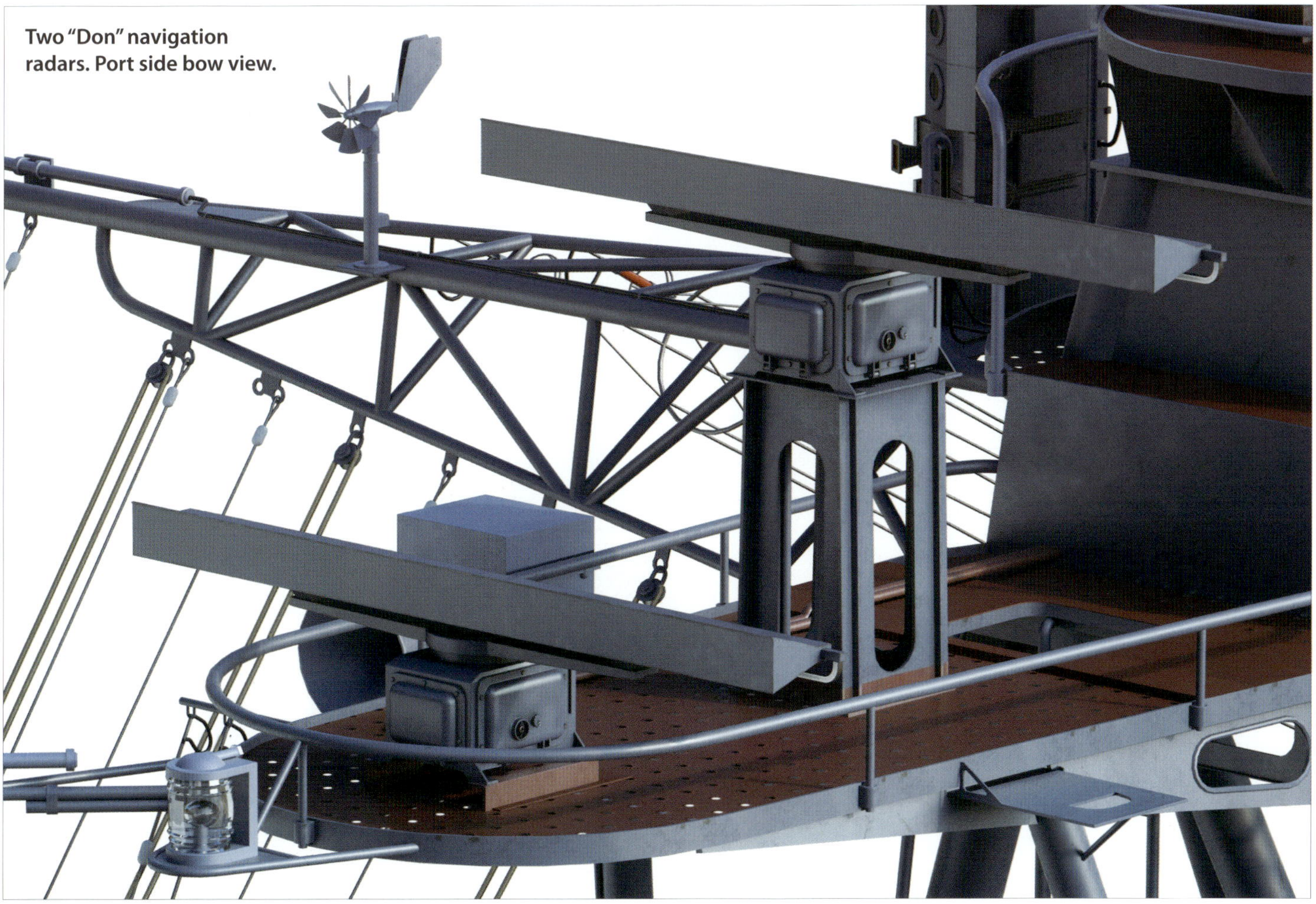

Two "Don" navigation radars. Port side bow view.

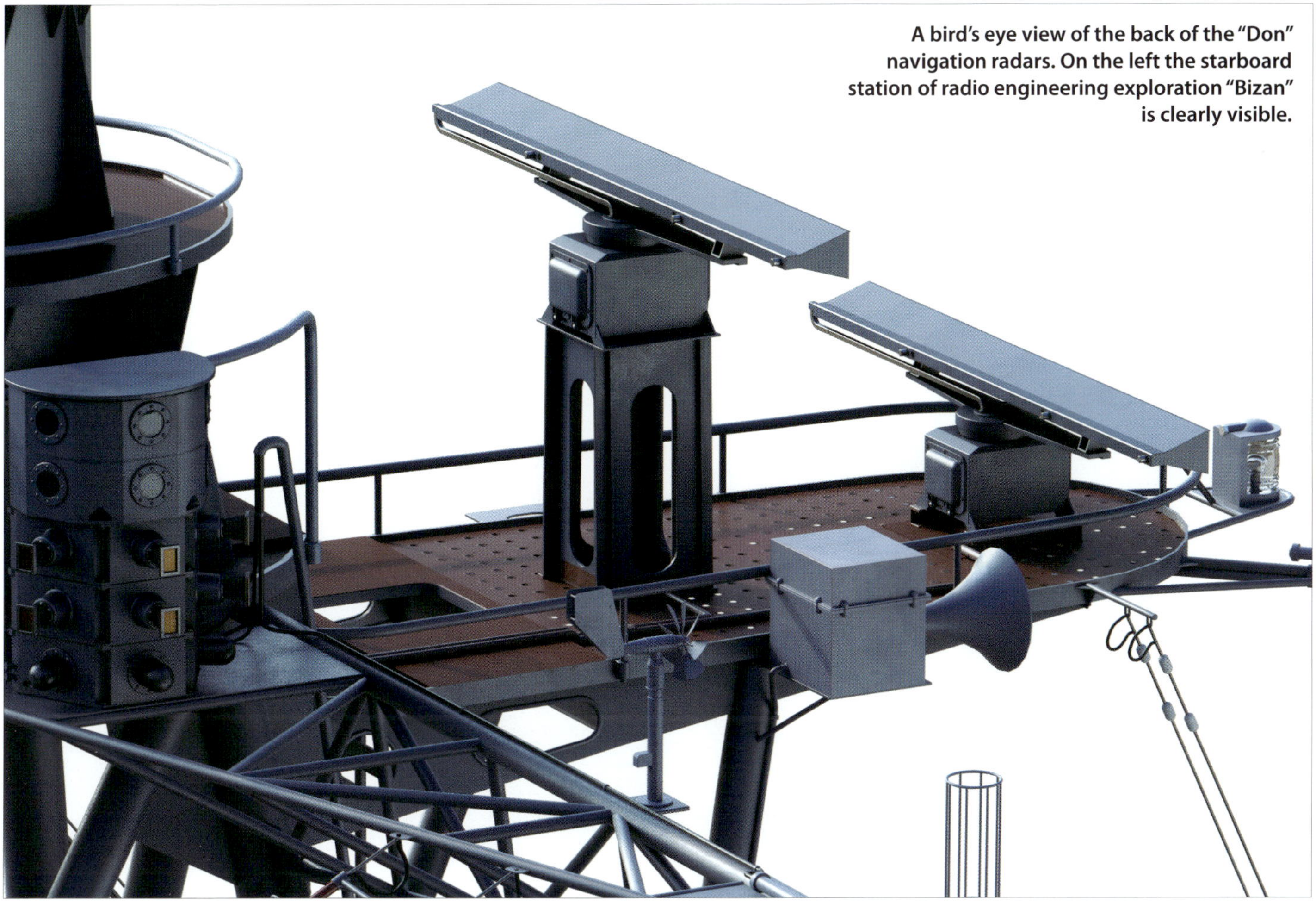

A bird's eye view of the back of the "Don" navigation radars. On the left the starboard station of radio engineering exploration "Bizan" is clearly visible.

The face of the port side MR-300 "Angara" target detection radar.

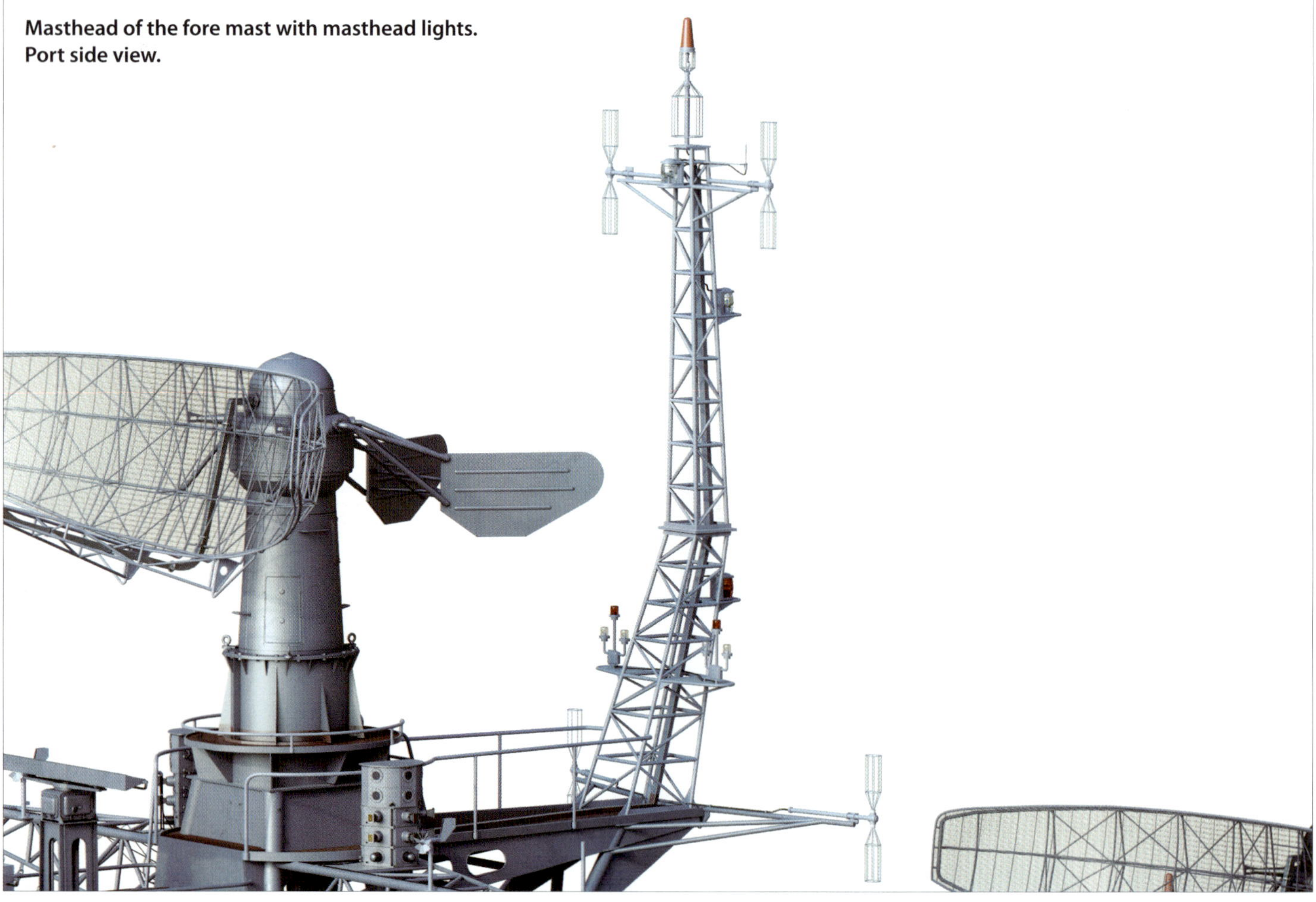

Masthead of the fore mast with masthead lights. Port side view.

The responder antenna of "Chrome-M" IFF system on top of the mast. (Identification Friend-or-Foe)

The base of the fore port side funnel seen from the port. The work cutter is visible in the foreground.

Same place, but without a work cutter.

Space between the foremast and the bow funnels. At the base of the fore mast there is the air intake for the ship's gas turbine engine.

Space between the foremast and the bow funnels. At the base of the fore mast there is the air intake for the ship's gas turbine engine.

Starboard view of the location of the commander cutter & the base of bow funnels.

The same viewpoint, but without commander cutter.

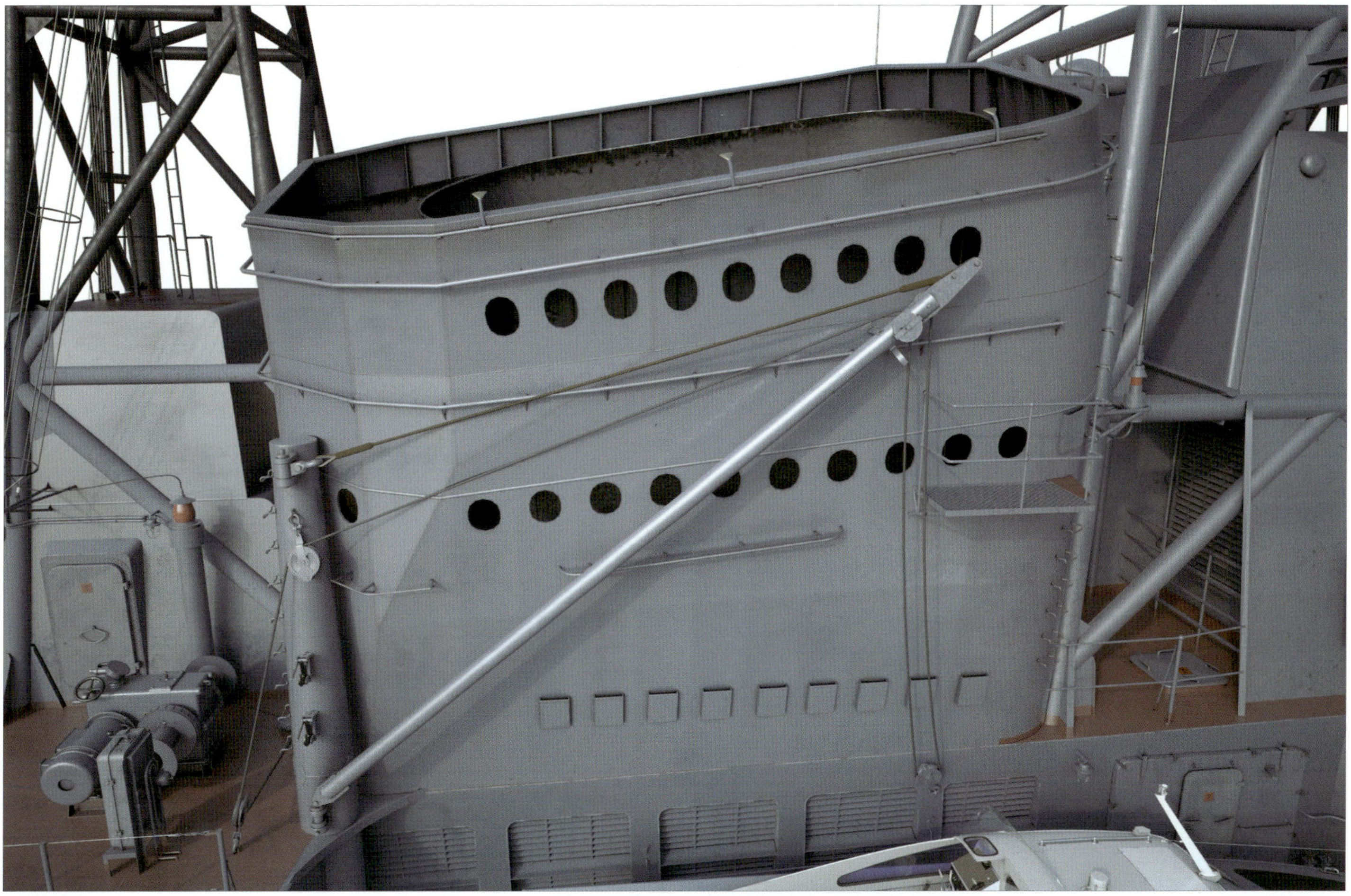

The starboard bow funnel.

A bird's eye view of the back of the starboard bow funnel.

View of the commander cutter stern from the main deck. Stern view.

Rear view of the starboard bow funnel and right winch. View from the superstructure deck.

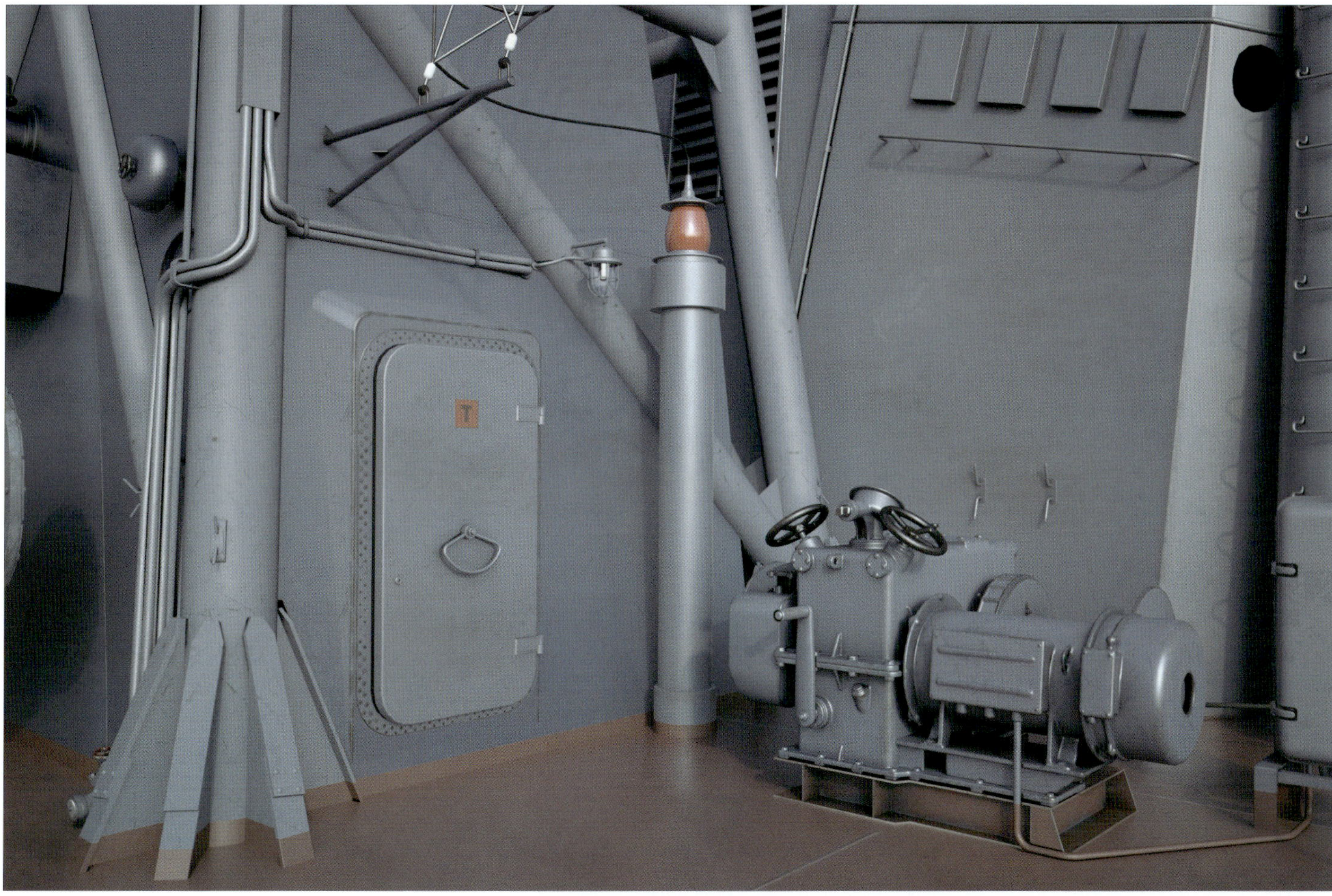

Starboard side view of the main mast base & right winch.

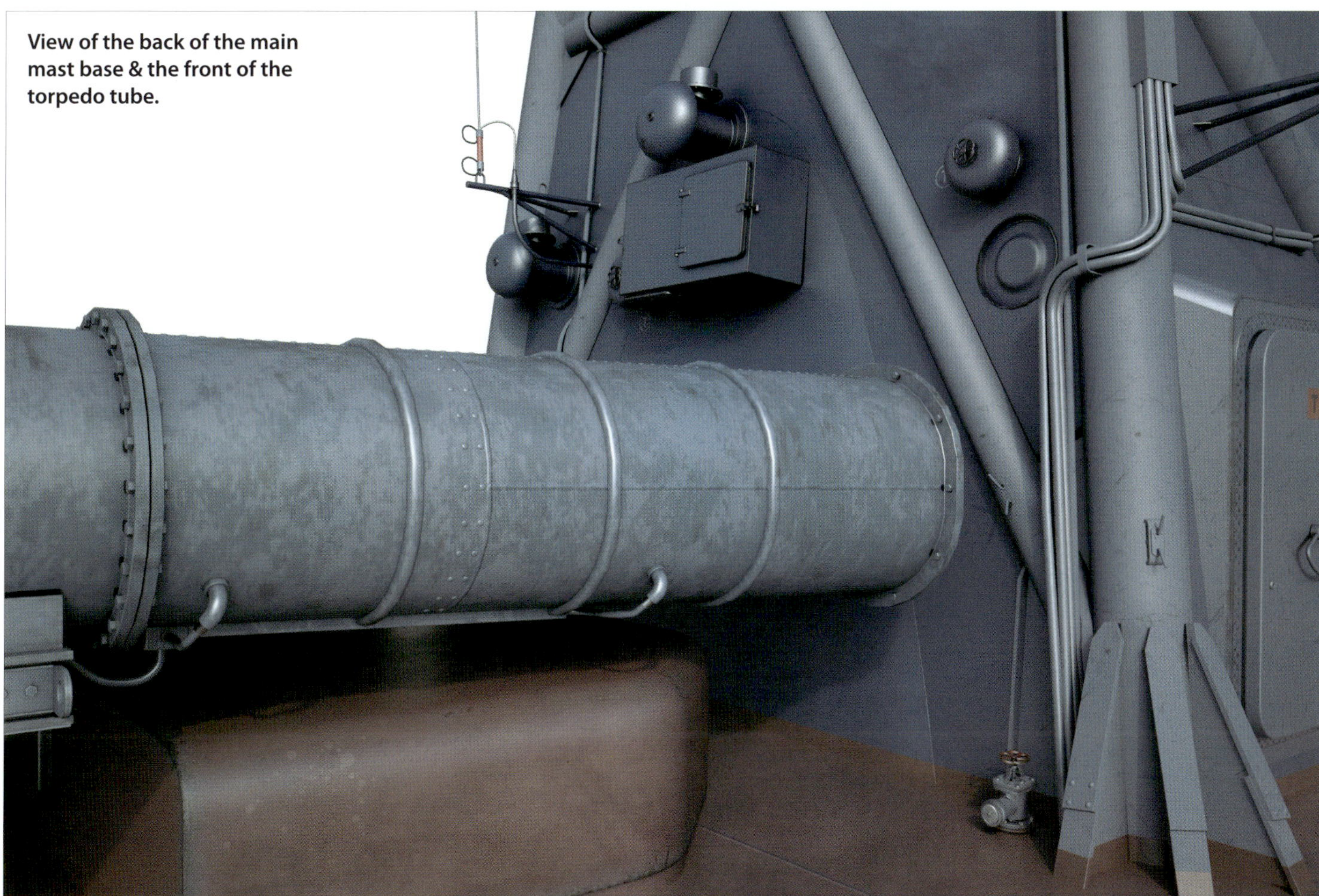

View of the back of the main mast base & the front of the torpedo tube.

Port side stern view of the main mast base & port side winch.

A bird's eye view of the work cutter stern. Stern view.

The base of the main mast seen from the port stern.

The upper tiers of the main mast with "Crab -M" antenna posts.

Second MR-300 " Angara" target detection radar of the main mast seen from the port stern. Right behind the radar, there is the second antenna of "Chrome-M" IFF system.

Port side view of the central section of the ship's superstructure, the base of the main mast and the torpedo tube.

Port side view from above on the torpedo tube, stern tower structure base.

Port side rails for torpedo loading cart.

Device for manually turning a torpedo tube when the torpedoes loading. Starboard side view.

The PTA 53-61 torpedo launcher. Port side view from above.

A bird's eye view of the back of the port side RBU-1000 depth charge rocket launcher.

Starboard side stern view of starboard RBU-1000 depth charge rocket launcher.

A bird's eye view of the stern tower structure. On the sides of the tower are visible antenna posts "Crab-M".

The upper part of the tower structure with a second stern "Yatagan" 4R-90 missile control radar.

Port side view of six-oars yal on the gravity davit. Air intake and port side stern funnel is visible in the background.

A bird's eye view of the stern funnels & second post of the stern MR-105 "Turel" artillery radar.

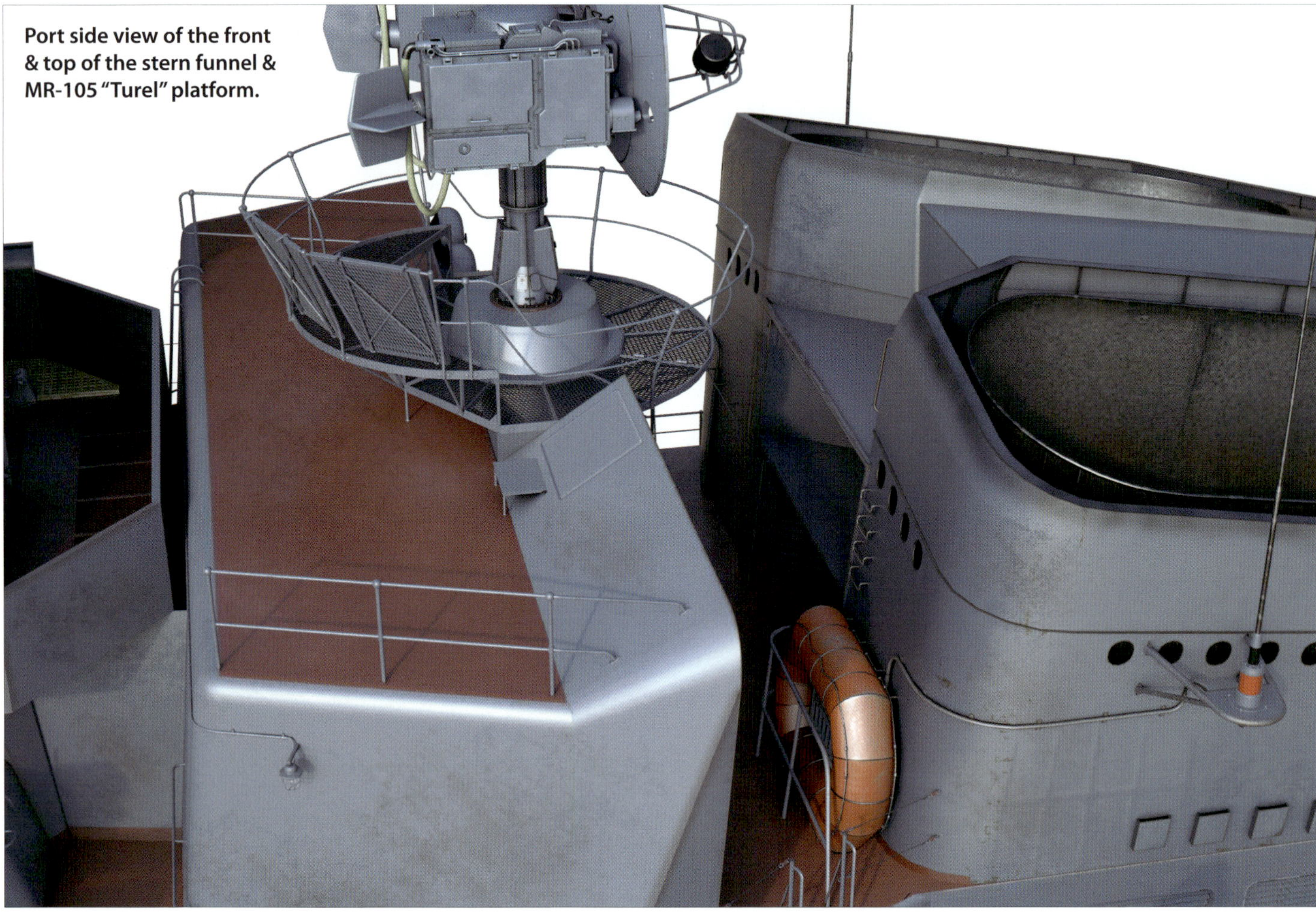

Port side view of the front & top of the stern funnel & MR-105 "Turel" platform.

The space in front of the stern funnels. Starboard side.

Starboard side, unfolded ladder.

A bird's eye view of the back of the stern funnels.

A bird's eye view of the stern funnels & the stern M-1 "Volna" anti-aircraft missile launcher.

The folded ladder of the port side.

Starboard side view of the stern M-1 "Volna" anti-aircraft missile launcher & the stern part of the superstructure.

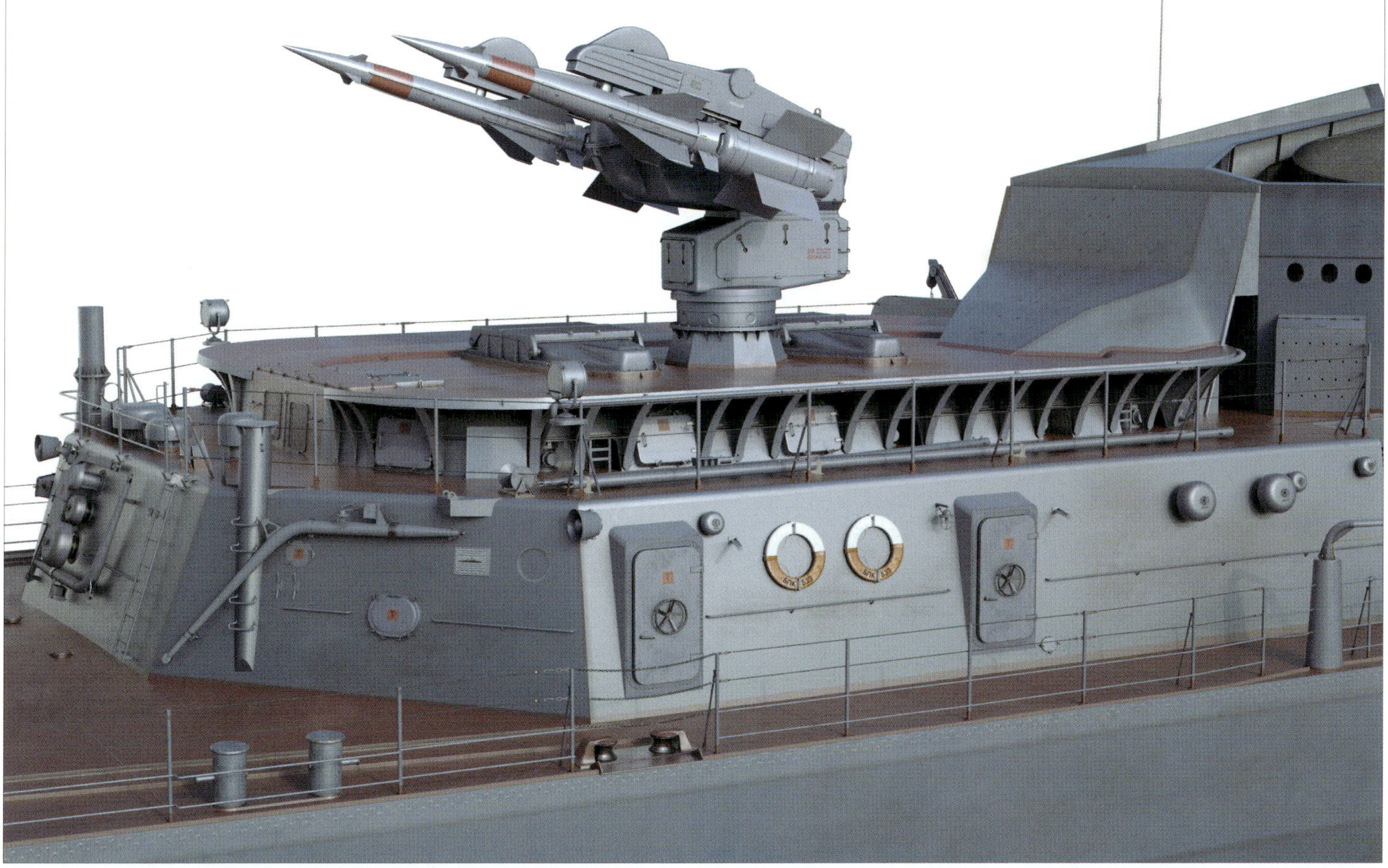

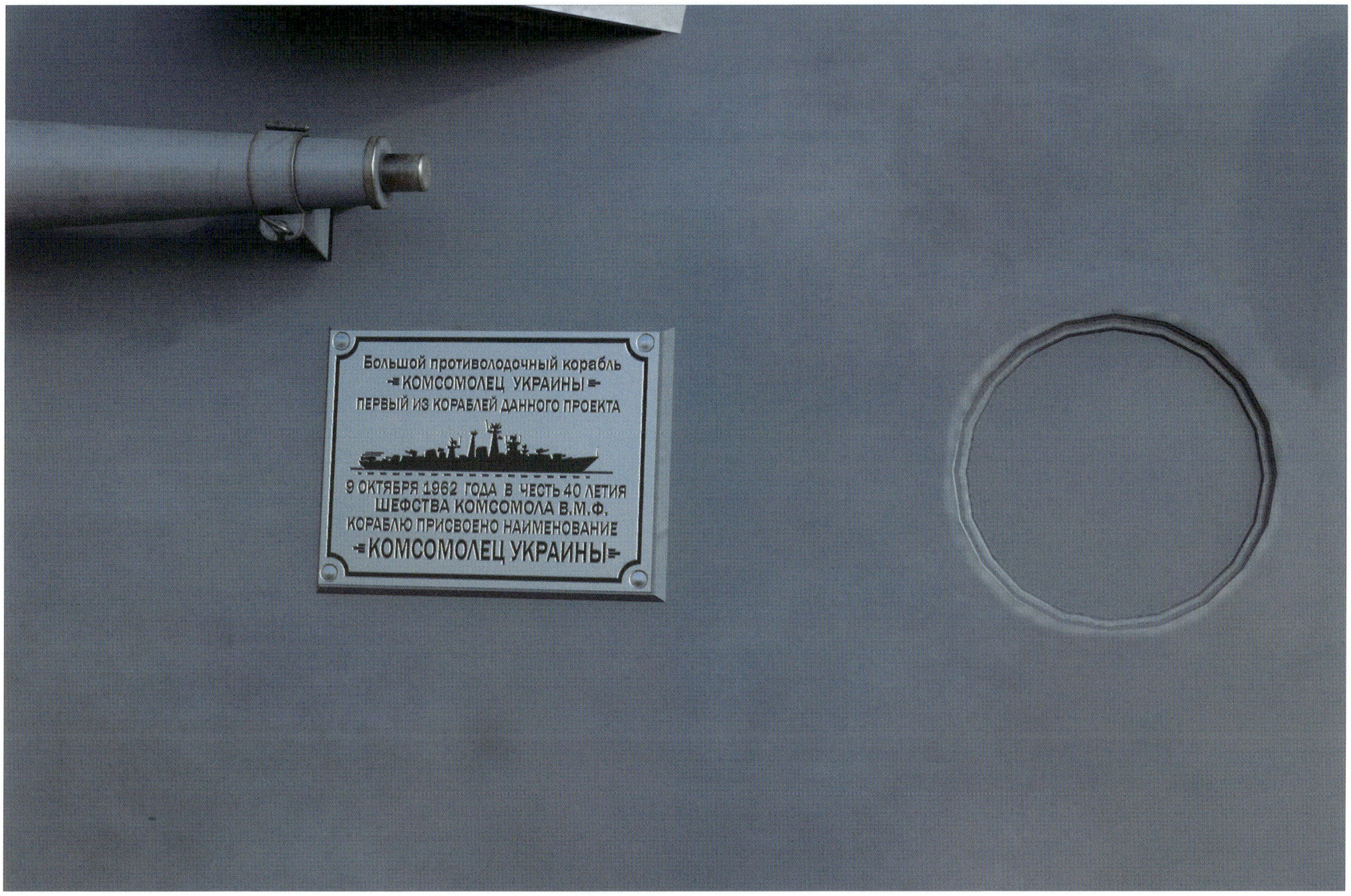

Commemorative plaque about giving the name of the ship.

A fragment of the rear part of the superstructure. Starboard side view.

The rear part of the superstructure. Port side view.

Port side of the back part of the superstructure. In the center the beam for rockets loading is visible.

The rear end of the ship's superstructure seen from the port astern.

Stern AK-726 turret. Port side view.

Launch/command post of the helicopter. Port side bow view.

The port side capstan control panel. Looking from the bow towards control panel.

Launch/command post of the helicopter. Port side view.

Launch / command post of the helicopter seen from the starboard stern.

Stern of the ship with the helipad seen from the starboard bow.

Stern of the ship with the helicopter on board. When the helicopter landing and taking off, the flagpole lowers.

Port view of the ship stern.

View on the stern.

W-601 rocket.

Rocket first stage. Rear view.

A lock connecting the first and second stages of the rocket.

Second stage of the rocket.

Warhead.

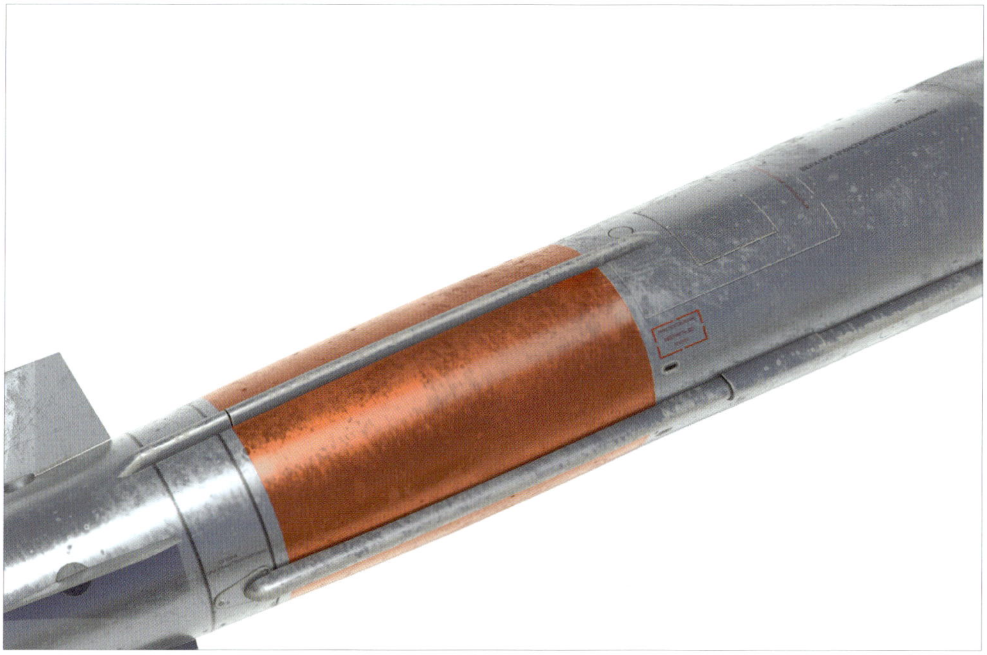

Warhead.

Rocket details.

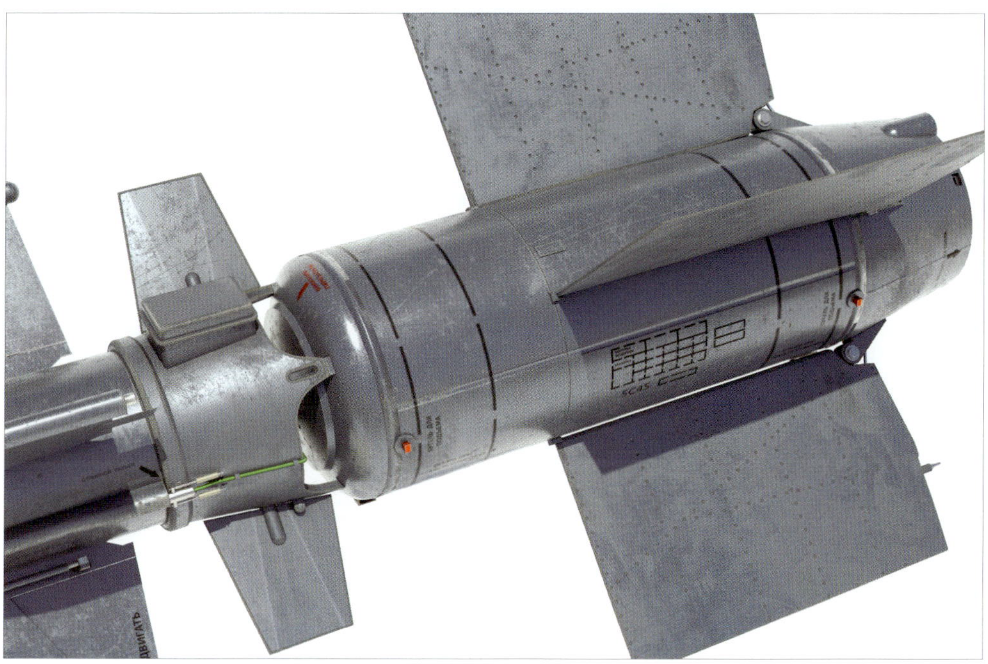

Rocket details.

Port side view M-1 "Volna" anti-aircraft missile launcher .

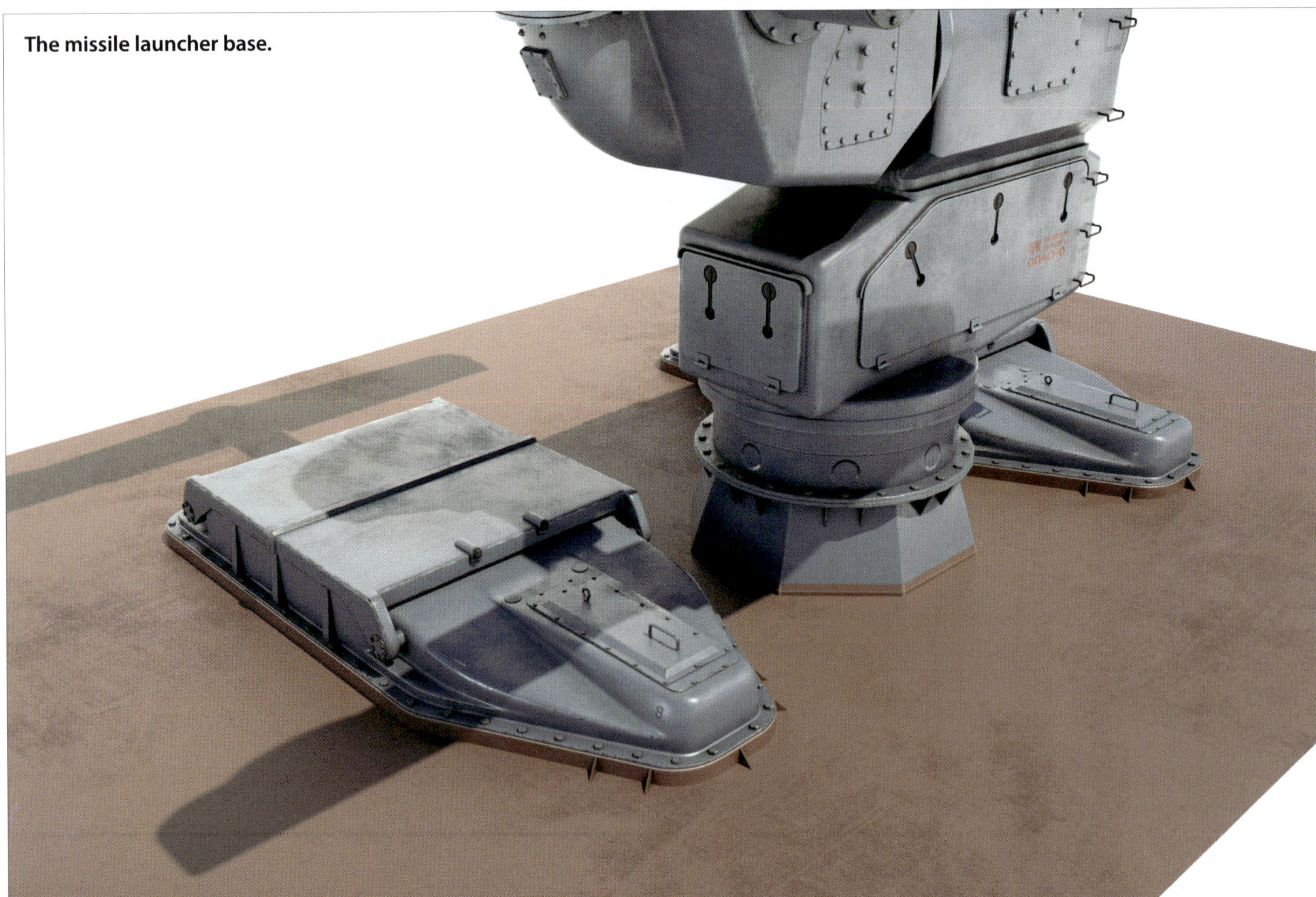

The missile launcher base.

Top view of the missile launcher.

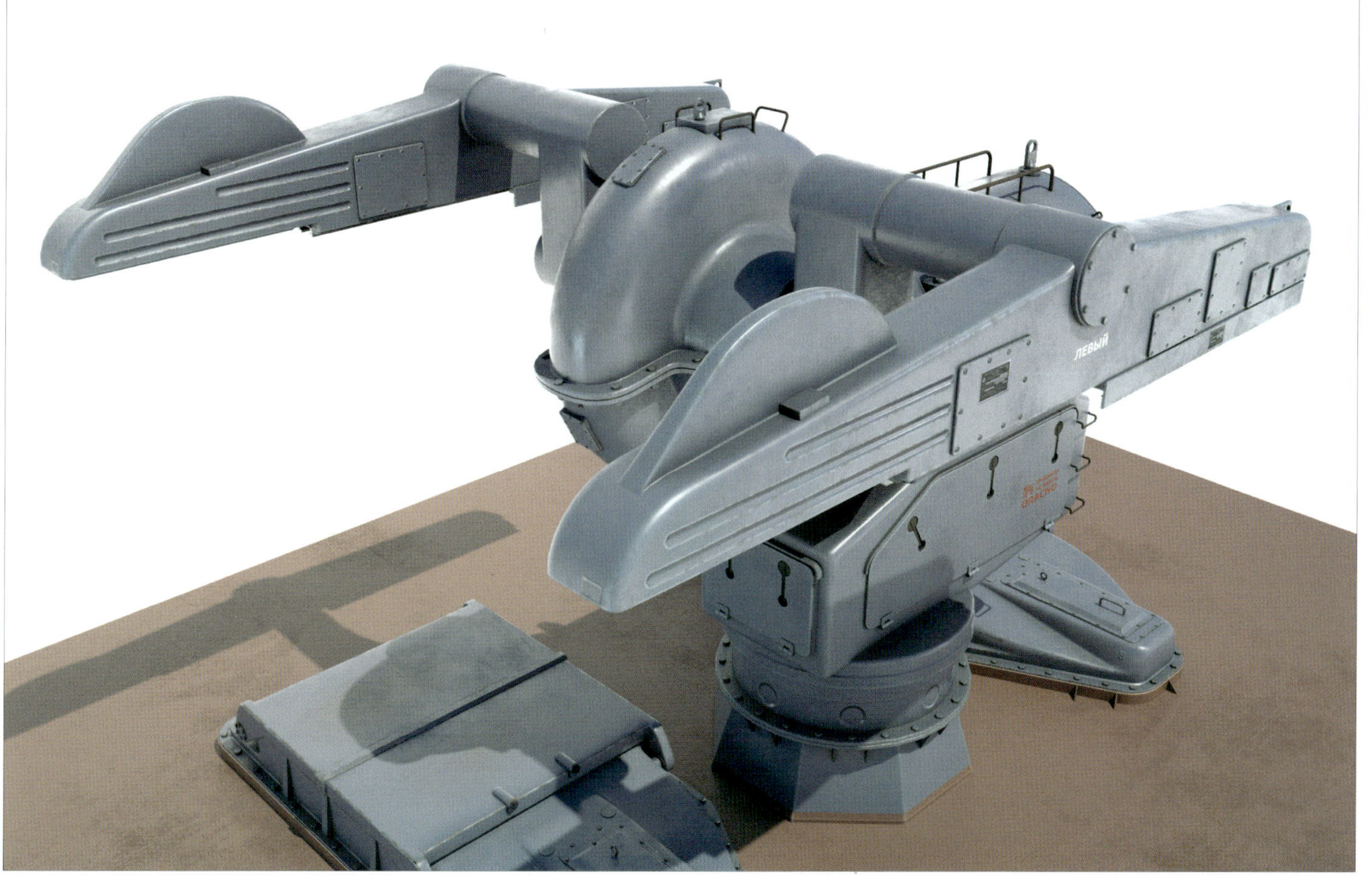

The missile launcher back view.

RBU-1200 depth charge rocket launcher & rocket.

Rear view of the RBU-1000.

Rear view of the RBU-1000.

300mm RBU rocket.

300mm RBU rocket.

MR-105 "Turel" artillery radar. Front left view.

MR-105 "Turel". Back left view.

Back view.

Front right view.

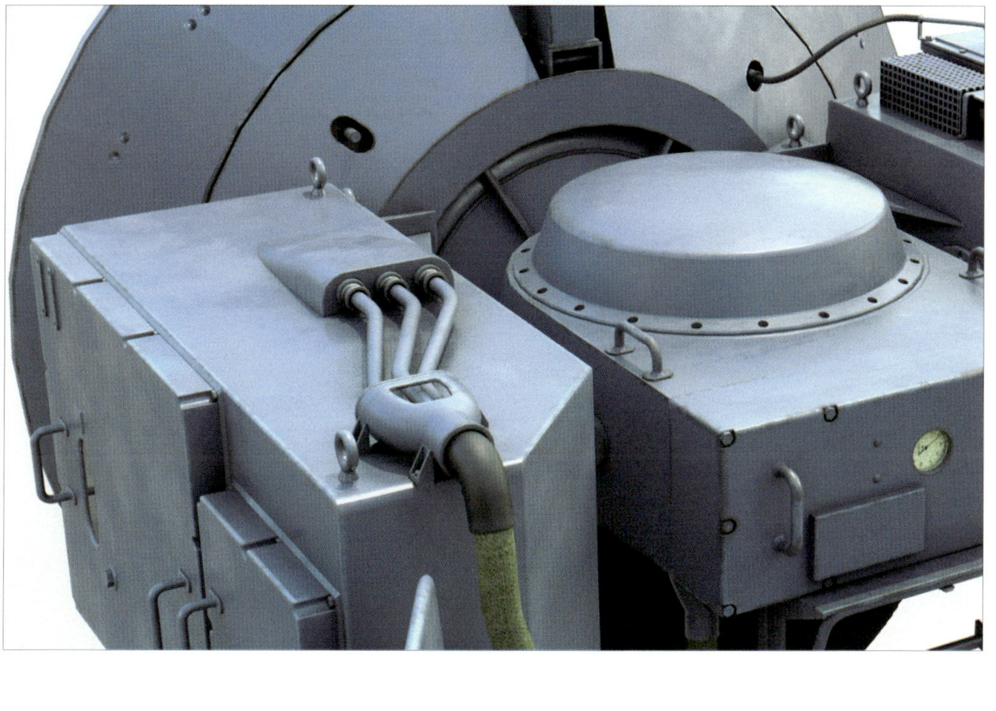

MR-105 "Turel" details close up.

Project 338 work cutter.

Universal 76mm twin gun AK-726 turret.

AK-726 turret back right view.

AK-726 turret front view.

AK-726 turret with the maximally raised barrels.

Commander cutter Proj. 1389.

Cutter seen from the stern.

Cutter seen from the bow.

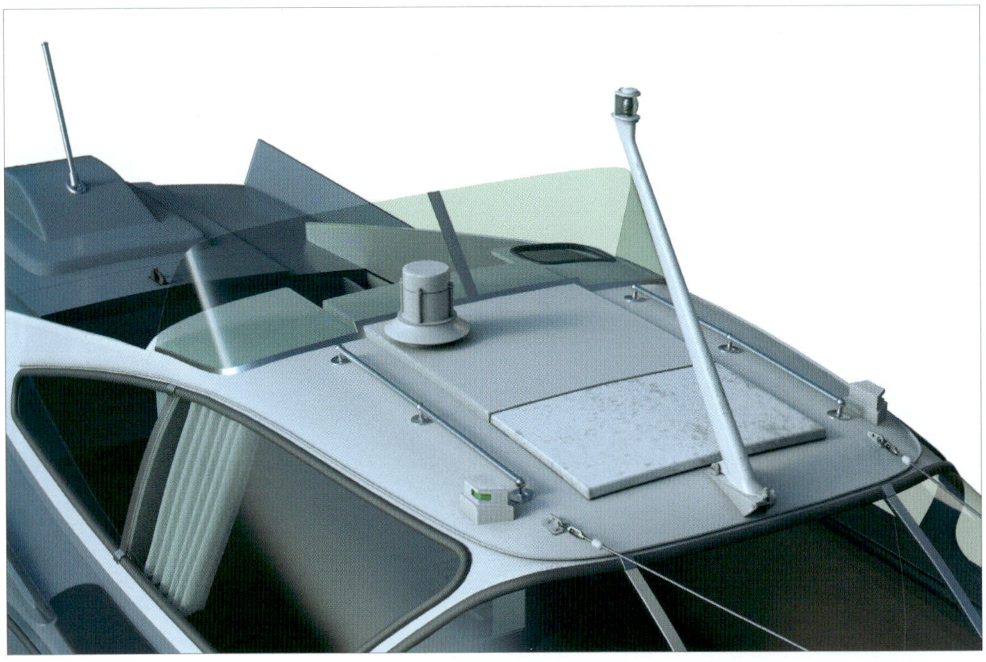

Cutter seen from the top.

Cutter interior.

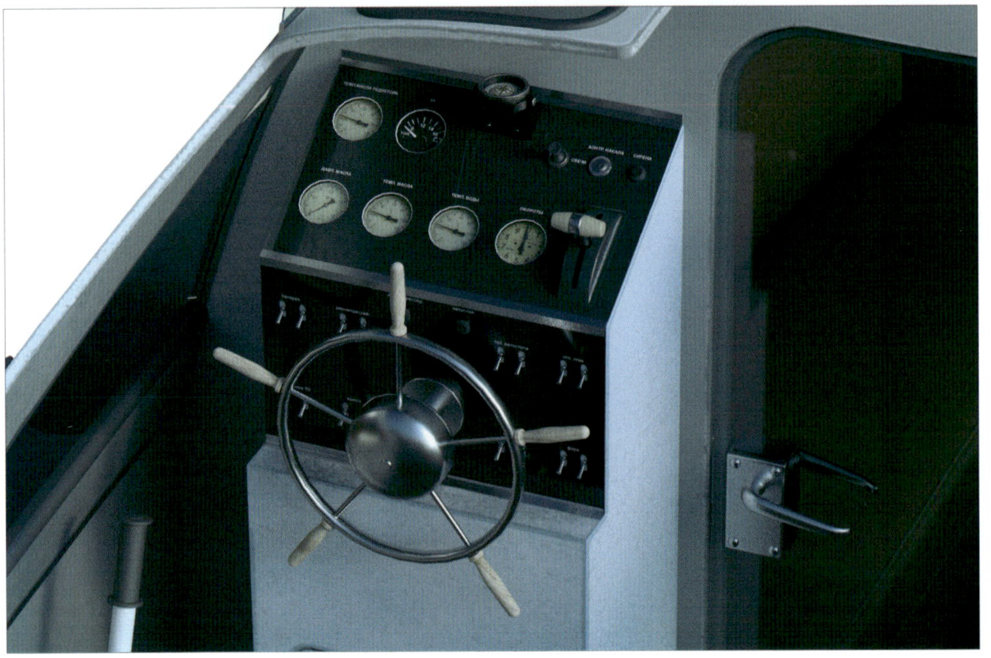

Instrument panel of the cutter.

PTA 53-61 torpedo launcher.

Back right view.

RBU-6000 depth charge rocket launcher.

RBU-6000 front right view.

MR-300 "Angara" target detection radar.

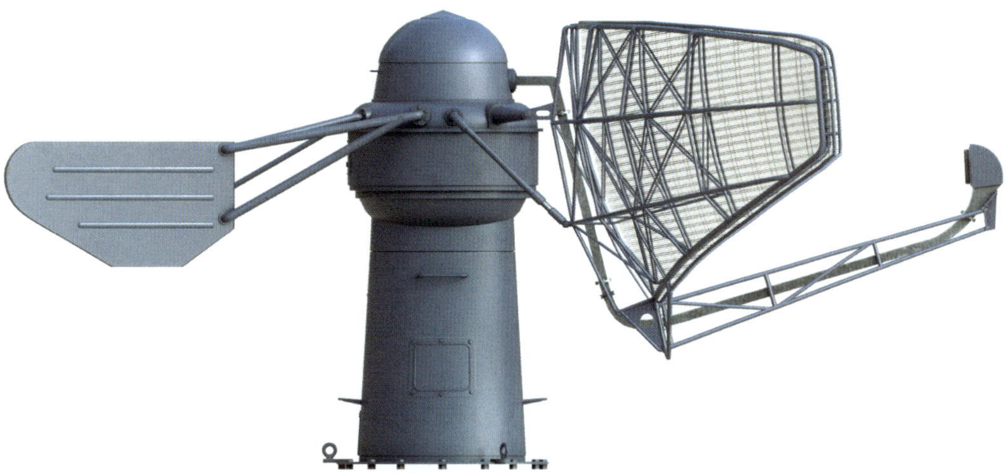

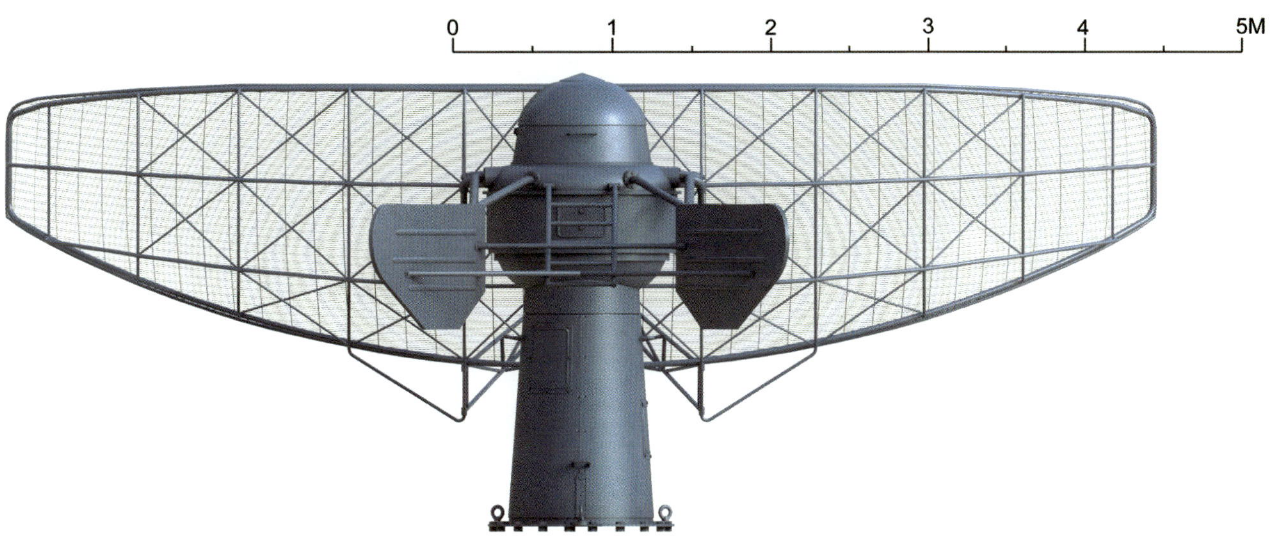

MR-300 "Angara" target detection radar.

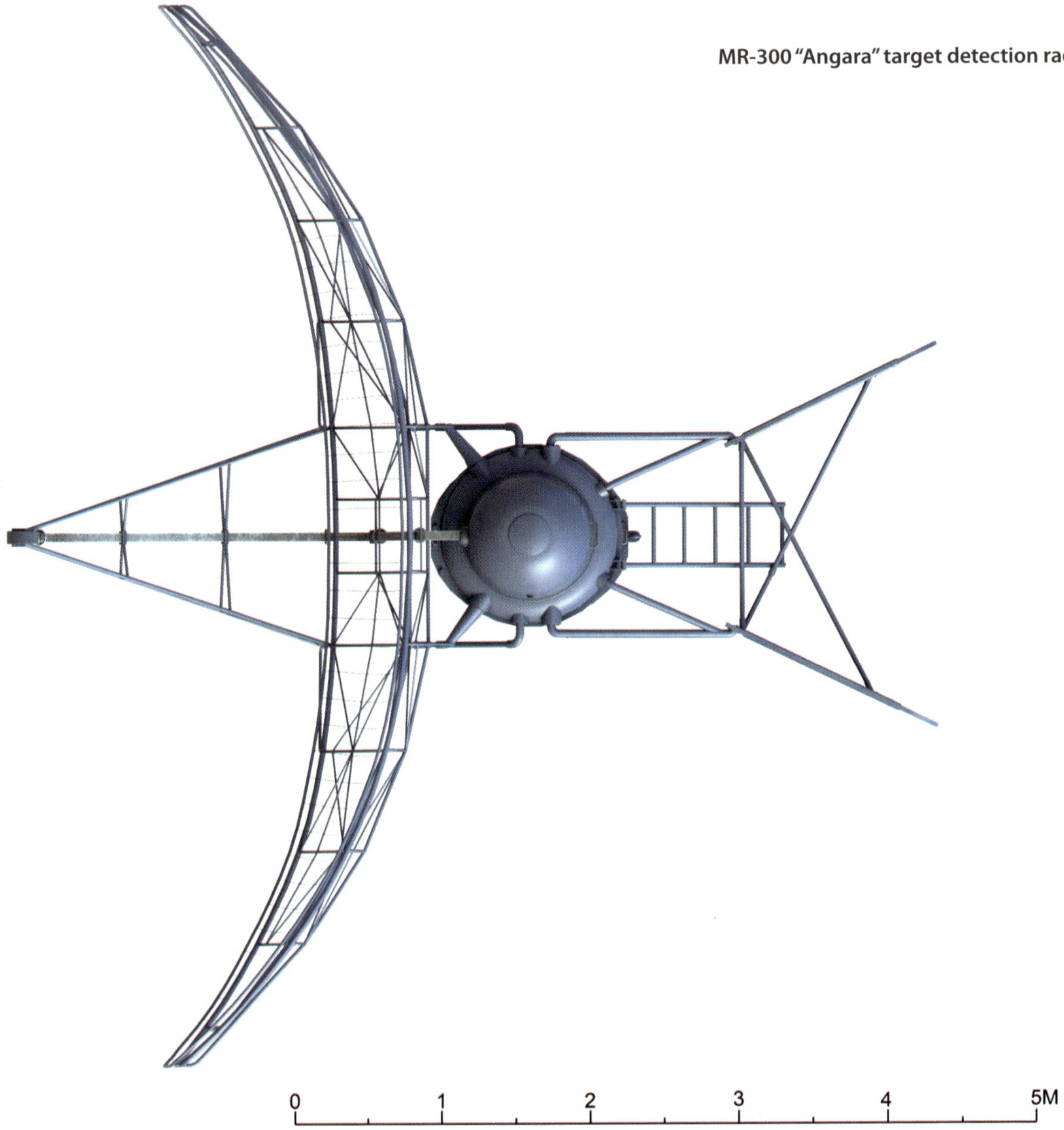

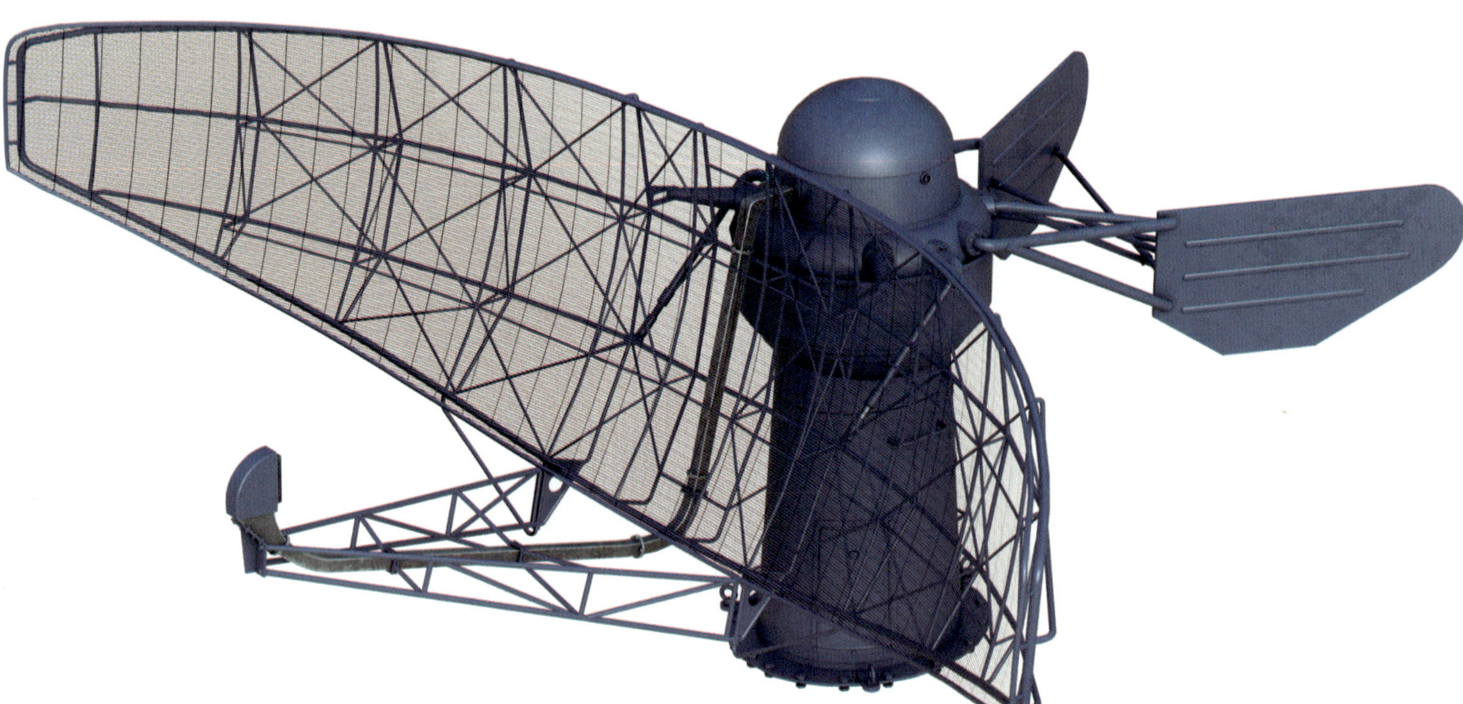

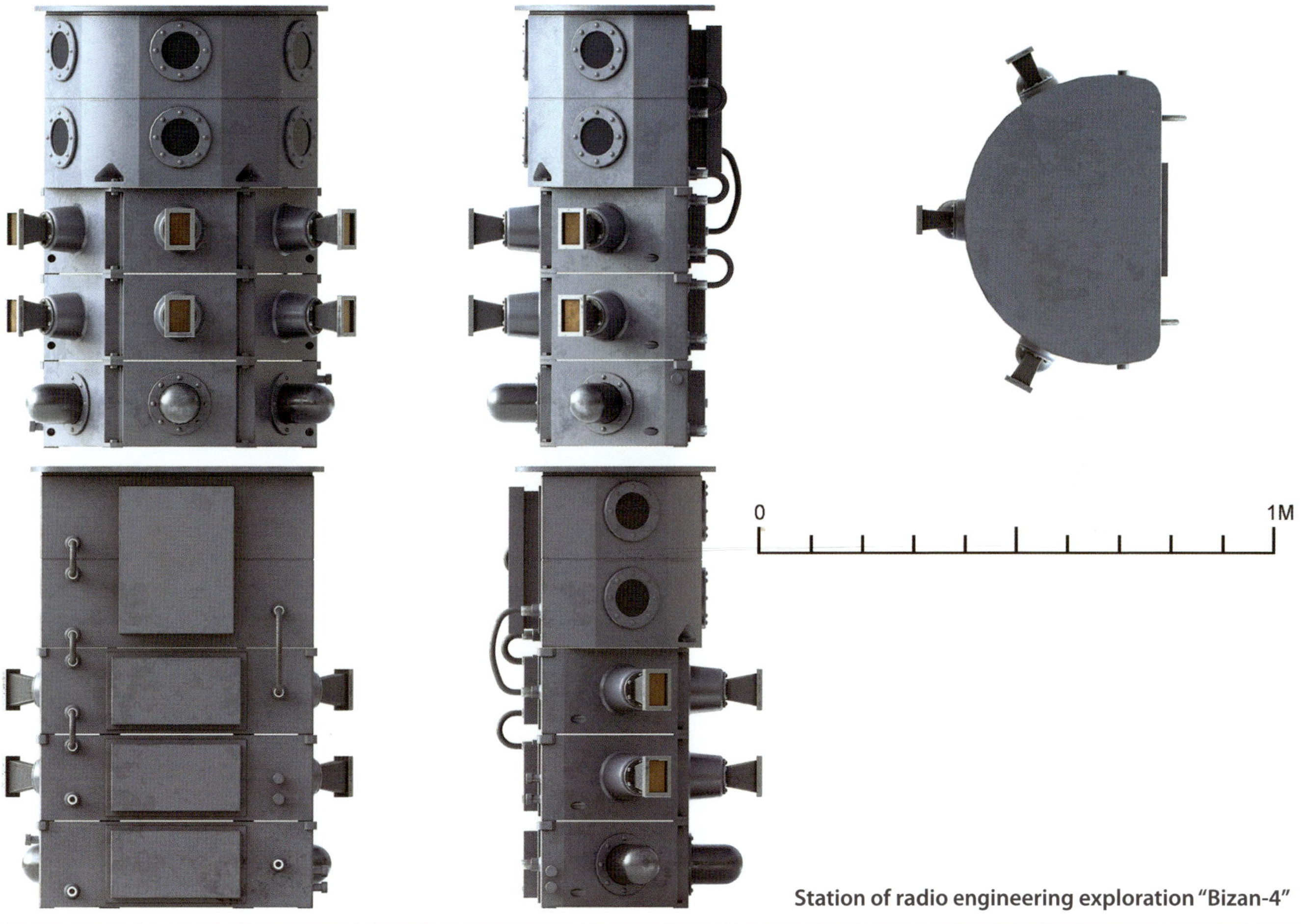

Station of radio engineering exploration "Bizan-4"

"Yatagan" 4R-90 missile control radar.

The passive jamming F-82-T mortar.

Front view of the F-82-T mortar.

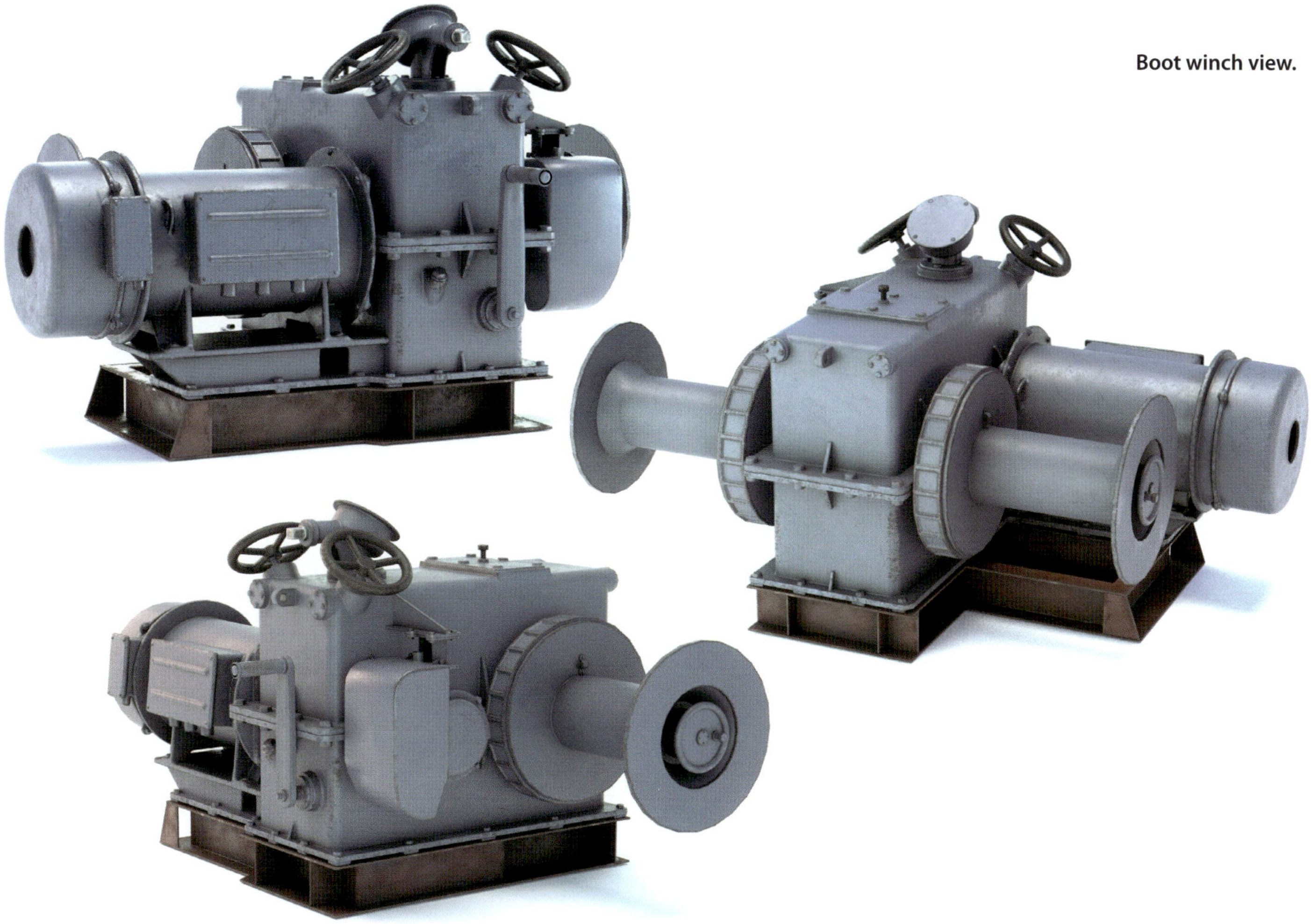

Boot winch view.

Six-oars yal view.

The Russian Missile Destroyer of Project 61 (Kashin Class) 1962 – Oleg Pomoshnikov

LUBLIN 2020 • ISBN 978-83-66148-67-3

3D illustrations and captions: **Oleg Pomoshnikov** • Text: **Jan Radziemski** • Translation: Stanisław Powała-Niedźwiecki (text) • Proofreading: Stanisław Powała-Niedźwiecki • Design: **KAGERO STUDIO** – Łukasz Maj

KAGERO Publishing • www.kagero.pl, e-mail: kagero@kagero.pl, marketing@kagero.pl

Editorial office, Marketing, Distribution: KAGERO Publishing, Akacjowa 100, os. Borek, Turka, 20-258 Lublin 62, Poland, phone/fax (+48) 81 501 21 05

w w w . k a g e r o . e u

The publishing house would like to thank Mr. Radziemski for all remarks regarding the books of the Super Drawings in 3D series and help in editing them.

3D visualisations are based on the available photographs, drawings and other archive data, and should be treated only as author's attempt to recreate the original look of the particular machine as faithfully as possible. If you are in possession of materials to which author did not reach, and you would like to help us to develop a better publication, please contact the Publisher on: redakcja@kagero.pl